BEYOND
THE HORIZON

Janice McLeod

Trilogy Christian Publishers, Tustin, CA

Trilogy Christian Publishers
A Wholly Owned Subsidiary of Trinity Broadcasting Network
2442 Michelle Drive Tustin, CA 92780

First Trilogy Christian Publishing hardcover edition October 2018

Cover design by Jeff Summers from Toward Something Creative Design Studio (towardsomethingcreative@gmail.com)

Trilogy Christian Publishing/ TBN and colophon are trademarks of Trinity Broadcasting Network.

For information about special discounts for bulk purchases, please contact Trilogy Christian Publishing.

Manufactured in the United States of America

10 9 8 7 6 5 4 3 2 1

Library of Congress Cataloging-in-Publication Data is available.

ISBN: 978-1-64088-183-9

ISBN: 978-1-64088-184-6 (eBook)

CONTENTS

ACKNOWLEDGMENT

Thanks to many dear friends and family who over the years have encouraged me to follow my dreams and creative bent to write short stories. Your love and support has been inspiring to me.

Feeling obscure, if not invisible, Jack Solomon has a secret treasure hidden within him, a marvelous gift from God. Over time, through a surprising brush with death, his amazing secret is revealed; and what was once a very private pursuit becomes a public treasure and wonderful legacy for Jack's entire community. Read **Life in the Shadows,** and discover who Jack Solomon really is.

LIFE IN THE SHADOWS

$\mathcal{J}$ack Solomon was from all appearances your average, ordinary, work-a day-guy, plodding his way through the trenches of his mundane job as a paper-pushing clerk of the court, in the small rural town of Hemings where he lived. This bachelor that was now forty-seven, who lived all alone but for the companionship of a fat tomcat named Chester, resided in a small basement apartment on Commerce Street, and was for the most part, living a quiet, unobtrusive life under the radar of those around him.

Jack, whom had been shy and bookish as a youth, had failed to blossom over time and now as an adult, lived a narrow, constricted life, choosing to remain in his comfort zone, fending off the interest of others by his very appearance and behavior. Jack was an unimposing man of five feet eight inches, sporting a shiny skull cap on the top of his balding head that was fringed by thin wisps of graying hair and framed by two large ears that stood out like bookends on either side of his bony narrow face. His long, pointed nose, more like a beak, supported two thick panes of glass from which he peered, held at their station by worn wire frames, taped at one corner. His pale blue eyes often darted nervously from side to side or up and down when he was forced, in the course of his work day, to speak to others. His small overbite seemed to accentuate his weak receding chin that sometimes quivered as he scampered around muttering about his to-do list.

The two pairs of gray and brown polyester pants he had worn for years were the staples of his meager wardrobe and were routinely coordinated with the same three shirts: one yellow, one blue, and one white to be highlighted with his ever-present green and maroon paisley bowtie. During the cooler months of the year, there was the addition of another fashion accessory; the standard tan sweater vest he put on faithfully to ward off the cold from his skinny, slight, frame. Now to imply that Jack was a slave to fashion was the standard joke in the office. Yes, being somewhat less than attractive, dressing oddly, and lacking a modicum of social graces had assured Jack of the quiet, private life he desired and the only one he was really suited for.

Late one afternoon, as he walked up Main Street, he then turned right on to Commerce where he headed another two blocks in the direction of his studio apartment. It was the end of November and the windy chill in the air tugged at his trench coat as he made his way up the street, so he hurried along. Unlatching his door, he bent down to scoop up the mail that had been slipped through his door slot. Glancing up, he threw the mail on a nearby table, then reached down to stroke Chester, his cat, who had leapt from the back of Jack's old, worn recliner and now stood at his feet rubbing his pant legs.

The first time Jack saw Chester, he had been a starving, stray kitten peeking out from trash cans behind the apartment house one night. Jack saw him as he made his weekly pilgrimage, stuffing the refuse of his singular life into the large beat-up cans. That had been some eight years ago now. Jack remembered picking up the tiny kitten in the palm of one hand as it meowed and shook all over from hunger and cold. He had laughed at this small, mangy, ball of fluff as he gazed at its large startled eyes and oversized pointed ears and thought how much this cat actually resembled him. Tucked into a fold at the edge of his tan vest, Jack took the kitten inside for a warm saucer of milk. Wetting the tip of his finger he encouraged his new friend to suck and lick at the only food it had seen since it lost its mother. This was the beginning of a lasting friendship that seemed to be all either of them wanted or needed.

This particular November day, Jack had rushed home to grab his camera and dash back down to the town square just four blocks from his apartment, for he had seen something that caught his eye. He needed to be fast for the clouds were ever moving and the light was fading quickly. Giving Chester a final quick pat on the head, he left his friend standing alone as he ran back out the door. The streets

4

were all but deserted as Jack rested his arms on the railing of the old bandstand and positioned his viewfinder to frame a cluster of old brick buildings, their simple architecture now cast in bright highlights and deep shadows, flanked by large, ancient, hickory trees that silhouetted their naked nest of branches against the fiery sky. Darkening clouds hovered just above the horizon, catching the remains of sunlight that cast molten gold along their jagged edges and underbelly. Jack worked quickly from three or four different angles, clicking off shots in rapid succession, then, the light was gone. Taking in a deep breath, and placing his camera back in its case, he pulled on his gloves and shook his head smiling as he thought to himself, "How magnificent", then he made his way back home.

This time when the door was opened, Chester, who now sat in the dark, stayed on his perch at the top of Jack's recliner and watched Jack flip on a lamp, remove his coat, and put on a pot of coffee before Chester made a move. When Chester heard the refrigerator door open and saw the small glow from inside, he knew it was supper time. Jack muttered soothing chatter to the cat as he moved from place to place in his tiny kitchenette, reaching for Chester's bowl, finding the hand-held can opener and a spoon from the sink that was always used to scoop cat food from the can. Chester picked up the scent of chicken livers and pounced to the floor, running to his bowl that had been placed near the kitchen table where Jack now sat with his mug of coffee. Jack reached into the pocket of his coat that had been tossed over a nearby chair and fished out his small camera and checked the number of exposures. Over the course of several years, he had shot many pictures of almost anything that interested him: people, places, objects, and now it was time to develop this latest roll of film. In a long, narrow cupboard, around the corner of the kitchen, near the back door, was where Jack kept his chemicals. He had rigged a fold-out tabletop to hold his picture trays. It gave him great pleasure to see what had been captured that might help him with his main pursuit.

Winter that year had marched straight forward from November into December and was headed on a collision course with Christmas. No sooner had the turkey from Thanksgiving been partially digested, than Hemingites were geared up for Saint Nick, and the Presbyterians had the stable scene they donated to the city, out on the lawn in front of the city library. Holiday lights had been strung surrounding the square, a sign that the Christmas crash had officially started. But for the most part, this man and his cat lived through the hubbub, mostly unscathed by it all, and emerged out the other side in January, tucked away in their small garret on Commerce Street, wrapped in soft, silent folds of drifted snow. Except for his trudging to the court house, the short days and long nights of winter were passed in quiet solitude. Hours came and went without Jack's notice, as he sat in the corner of his small living room huddled near the room's only window and source of natural light. He had set up a workstation there, a place to put his supplies and a comfortable, worn, upholstered armchair, where Chester could nest quietly on its tall back and watch his friend Jack work his magic. A key ingredient to these prolonged work sessions was the presence of soft, beautiful music that Jack knew by heart and would often hum as he labored along. Chester also found the music comforting and inspiring in a feline way and would often swish his tail back and forth, leading the symphony through a particularly stirring piece. During small breaks, as Jack would sit back in his chair to survey his work, Chester would climb down over Jack's shoulder and rub Jack's chin with his head as he sat on his lap. Jack would then stroke Chester's back and ask his closest confidant for an honest evaluation of the work at hand. Chester honored their close friendship and would always manage a reply of meowing and pawing on Jack's chest to which Jack would reply, "I thought you would say that!"

Now, as is a natural course in life, one cold, windy Tuesday in February, Jack didn't feel so well. His complaint of chest pain and shortness of breath had started in the middle of the night and had only slightly abated by 9:00 a.m. the next morning when he phoned his office to say he would not be in that day. As Jack lay silent in his bed, Chester nervously patrolled the apartment knowing something was very wrong with his friend Jack, whose face now shone with perspiration in the pale glow of the morning light. What was a cat to do in a situation like this? He jumped up in the window sill and peered out anxiously but saw no help coming. Next, he leaped up on the counter in the kitchen and licked at the occasional drip coming from the faucet. Rushing back to Jack's bedside, Chester stood on Jack's chest with watchful eyes but no hand was raised in the usual morning salvoes of attention and affection. Something had gone very wrong.

When the office at the courthouse heard no further word concerning their absent employee, an inquiry was made several times by phone with no response. Finally, after three days, Jack's supervisor, Ted

Dawson came around to his apartment and with the apartment manager in tow, they used a master key to enter the apartment after several rapid knocks on the door went ignored. When they opened the door, there was an odd odor permeating the air that strangely smelt like linseed oil. In the half light of his tiny, cluttered apartment, Jack was lying in his bed as he had been for the past few days and was unable to respond to the men who now called his name. Chester bolted to the door of Jack's bedroom as the two men approached. Finally spotting Jack, Ted was astonished to see the silent, frozen expression on Jack's face as he cast his eyes back and forth with a look of alarm but seemed otherwise unable to move or speak. The apartment manager, Allen Shaw, had seen something like this before and explained to Ted about his wife's mother who had a heart attack and stroke last spring that had left her partially paralyzed. With calm words of reassurance, Ted asked Jack if he could hear him, at which point Jack could only blink. Allen quickly took Jack's hand and told him they would call for an ambulance and get him some help at the regional hospital in Madison. Chester again pounced up on the bed and rubbed Allen's hand that now held Jack's.

Allen patted the nervous cat and said, "The poor thing must be starved." He momentarily left Jack's bedside and went to the kitchen.

As the two men waited for the medics to arrive, they tried to reassure Jack that help was on the way and that Chester would be taken care of. Having a few moments to catch their breath and gather their thoughts, the two men began surveying their surroundings. To their total amazement, they saw beautiful oil paintings of all kinds covering the walls in every room and more stacked in the corners here and there. How totally unexpected this was! There were also piles of colored photographs strewn here and there with a few stuck to a corresponding painting of the same subject. Near the front corner window in the living room was a beautiful painting in progress arranged on a table easel. It was surrounded by oil paints, a wide variety of brushes stuck in an oversized coffee mug and two bottles of linseed oil with some still resting in a small tin cup near an old wooden pallet. The painting was exquisite in its dynamic coloring and life-like detail. The work being rendered was a large, crystal bowl of hot pink cabbage roses with a rounded, plump dew drop running off the edge of one delicate petal. A Japanese fan was partially flared out in front of the bowl of flowers along with a finely tooled, gold filigreed matchbox. All of these items were artfully arranged on a rich, brown velvet shawl with draping fringe, the entire scheme set slightly skewed. Pushed up against one short wall in the living room was a rustic cupboard that housed an ancient record player and several old LPs of mostly symphony music, some Gershwin and the old masters of the classics.

Ted looked at Allen in total shock and asked if he knew that Jack was a fine artist, to which Allen replied, "No, I haven't been in this apartment since renting it to Jack some eighteen years ago!"

Ted shook his head and felt a bit embarrassed and ashamed that he had never given this man a second thought as they worked side by side for so many years. Just as he was dealing with his own mixed emotions, there was a knock at the door and the EMT responders were let in by Allen. Quickly moved on to a gurney, with all vital signs checked and noted, Jack was whisked away in the ambulance, leaving Allen and Ted standing there in the quiet apartment, with Chester looking on from the back of Jack's recliner. As the two men walked to the front door and then outside, Allen turned to Ted as he locked the door and asked if Jack had insurance through his work.

Ted replied, "Yes, there was a general benefit package offered to all employees and I'm sure Jack would have taken advantage of that."

The two men clasped hands and vowed to stay in touch until this situation with Jack was resolved, then they parted company. As Ted climbed into his car, he shook his head in amazement and said to himself out loud, "You really can't tell a book by its cover!"

Now in the weeks that followed, it was determined that Jack had indeed suffered a mild heart attack and stroke. During his hospital stay, he received visits from both Ted and Allen. To Jack's total amazement, Ted actually appeared one afternoon with a potted plant and a card signed by courthouse staffers. Jack, who had no real work relationships, did not know how to react to this gesture, but nonetheless uttered a somewhat contorted thanks. What Jack didn't realize was that his cover had been blown and that Ted had shared information about him with his coworker while they sat in their Monday morning meeting. Not only did he give them an update on Jack's physical condition but also the most wondrous and surprising news of all, that Jack was a fabulous, highly skilled fine artist. Ted explained that he felt bad that Jack had been the butt of jokes over the years and that no one including himself, seemed willing or able to look beyond the obvious with this man to see if there was something more. Ted said he was determined to make an effort with Jack in the future and hoped that the staff would do likewise. They would all need to wish Jack a speedy recovery and show him some kindness and patience when he returned to work.

As Jack now looked to be released from the hospital, home healthcare aids were scheduled to attend to him as he groped into an uncertain future toward recovery and rehabilitation. Allen, who had taken charge of Chester in Jack's absence, was at the hospital the morning Jack was released to drive him home. The moment the door to Jack's apartment was opened, Chester dashed to his friend's side, meowing and swishing his tail around his legs with joyous zeal. Instantly scooped up into Jack's arms, the fat tomcat rubbed his head on Jack's face and licked at his cheek. Allen smiled as he put down a small bag of Jack's personal belongings and watched their affectionate reunion, commenting that he knew they both had really missed each other and how nice it would be for them to settle back into their old routine. Jack was slightly paralyzed on his left side and his mouth drooped slightly, making the formation of some words sound slurred, but his attitude was good and he was determined to march forward with his life no matter what that might look like. He was happy to be alive and home with Chester.

Later that first evening back in his apartment, Jack and Chester snuggled up together in the old, upholstered armchair by the window and listened to the soft melody of Pachelbel's Canon in G Minor, while bathed in the soft lamp light. Jack was wrapped in a red and blue plaid blanket with his feet on a small foot rest, while Chester sat square in Jack's lap curled in a ball with his eyes closed and motor purring. As Jack gazed across the apartment walls at the many paintings that chronicled his life, he was filled with a sense of love and gratitude for the ability God had given him, even though it appeared he might have been shorted in other areas. In Jack's mind, those other areas had been more than compensated for by the many years of immense joy and pleasure he had in observing the world around him, then painting it; thus in some small way claiming all those things for his own. So, he had lived a full, rich life vicariously through his paintings, if perception was anything.

By mid-April, Jack's health had improved some and being right-handed had helped him compensate for the loss on his left side. Rehab had helped him regain some of his strength and coordination, while a speech therapist had made great strides with his ability to form troublesome words. Throughout his slow recovery, Jack still heard from Ted and Allen, whom had for some reason taken an interest and liking to him. Both men routinely monitored his needs and made sure that the small necessities of life were attended to. On one such visit when Ted appeared with a basket of fresh fruit, the conversation that day led to the issue of sick leave that was about to expire. Ted was concerned about Jack's ability to return to work and asked about his plans. Jack explained that through his health crisis he had learned just how precarious and fleeting life could be and that in the quiet hours of his recovery, he had formulated another path forward for his life.

Ted was intrigued by this news and asked Jack what he had in mind. Jack told Ted he thought his return to work at the courthouse would be difficult and a slow go for the work that needed to be completed each day. He went on to say that being less than 100 percent, he tired easily and still had to lie down in the afternoon on the days he had therapy. He just didn't see when, in the near future, the situation might significantly change, so he was going to retire. Well, you could have knocked Ted over with a feather. Of all the things he thought might come out of this conversation, Jack's retirement was not even on his radar. Ted pressed on and asked Jack how he would get by for the long haul in case his impairment did not improve and then offered an enthusiastic, creative solution.

"Jack, have you ever thought about showing and selling some of your art work," Ted asked.

Jack seemed stunned by this idea and confessed that what he had painted through the years had been strictly for his own pleasure and that he never thought anyone else might be interested in his work.

Ted remarked, "Are you kidding? Your work is remarkable in its diversity and life-like detail. Why, any gallery would be proud to have even a single piece of your work!" Jack's face turned pink and flushed at Ted's comments, for he had never received any kind of praise or encouragement from another living soul for anything he had ever done.

Over the following weeks, Jack and Ted put their heads together and there was more talk about how to introduce Jack to the public and show some of his paintings. They thought to test the waters locally first, by having the *Hemings Gazette* do a story on Jack and then announce a one-man show that could be sponsored by the city library. "Hometown Hidden Treasure" was the headline of the story and featured a photo of Jack sitting at his easel, brush in hand, smiling. Soon after the article published, an art dealer from Memphis by the name of Henry Whaler was consulted and asked to market Jack's art for a reasonable profit margin. After seeing Jack's large inventory, Henry was amazed at the sheer volume and technical skill of Jack's work and suggested it all be cataloged and that a professional brochure be developed and sent out to galleries in the region. Henry also suggested that Jack enter his painting of *Geese Flying Over Snowden's Pond* in the Wild Life Painters Expo at the Pierce Art Center in Chicago, the grand prize being $25,000. With Ted as his front man and personal advocate and Jack's remarkable work speaking for itself, a new life and career was launched in a matter of weeks to the wonder and amazement of all. Jack, who had been scarcely known by anyone in the very town where he had lived for years, unwittingly became an overnight celebrity and favorite son.

What happened next to Jack was as surprising as the rest. At the pinnacle of his new success and notoriety in the art world and his own home town, Jack had not changed his humble lifestyle a single bit. After all, he was who he had always been, even if others seemed to see him differently now. He and Chester remained in their apartment on Commerce Street. The days came and went in regular succession and often soft, dreamy music echoed from the small apartment and a whiff of linseed oil could be detected in the air.

It was on a warm, sunny day in May, just eighteen months after Jack's heart attack, that a sweet spring breeze blew through the screen door and open windows of the apartment for the first time since the long, dark months of winter. Allen came by and rapped on the door frame to announce himself as he entered the apartment calling Jack's name. Seeing Jack's bald spot from the back of the recliner, he headed that way. As Allen sat down across from Jack on a small sofa, he rattled on about the event scheduled next week in the town square, the annual May Day Festival, and asked if Jack would want a tent set up to protect his artwork. When Jack didn't respond and just stared straight ahead like Allen wasn't there, his friend leaned forward to take a closer look at him. It was then Allen discovered Jack was dead. The gentle breeze that swirled through Jack's apartment that warm day in May had caressed his spirit and lured it away. The master artist and obscure town clerk danced in the moments of his life, through his gift of soulful art that gave such rich meaning to his paintings and had inadvertently left a legacy behind, a thumbprint that testified he had indeed existed.

In the weeks that followed, many in the town of Hemings were truly shocked and bewildered that this flaming nova that had surprisingly appeared in their midst had exited just as quickly. Ted for one seemed especially grieved by the loss. Jack, having no real family to speak of, had left the scraps and few details of his life in a file folder in the cupboard where he kept his music. Allen and Ted, Jack's closest friends took it upon themselves to handle the remaining business of Jack's life. To their astonishment, they discovered Jack had a sizable bank account and had designated the totality of his funds to be left to his cat Chester, through the governance of a trust to be managed by Allen until Chester expired. Any remaining money was to be dispersed to the local animal shelter and spent at their discretion. Jack had also left the remainder of his artwork to the City of Hemings, to be held in perpetuity as a memorial of his life once lived among them.

As Ted and Allen walked together from the Hemings Cemetery, they commented on the large turnout for the funeral and graveside service. The two men spoke again of the irony of Jack's quiet, sheltered life that in the end had touched so many people in such a wonderful and surprising way. Ted told Allen that one of the buildings Jack had painted a couple of years back, just off the town square, was now vacant and owned by the city. It had been decided in a city council meeting that the building would become the town's new welcome center and that one of the larger rooms would be designated to house Jack's gift to the city. The space was to be named the Jack Solomon Gallery of Fine Art. The two men smiled and laughed as they patted one another on the shoulder and shook hands that afternoon and went their separate ways. As Ted headed back to the courthouse, he marveled at how Jack's life had unintentionally made such an impact on their small rural community and how the beauty of his art would continue to touch lives for years to come. Jack had truly left the town a better place than when he found it. Ted gazed back toward the cemetery as he now coasted down Taylor Street and was again reminded of the lesson Jack had taught the town by his quiet example: that all people have intrinsic value and that all manifest the beauty of their quintessential elegance in many different ways.

"Rest in peace little buddy," said Ted. "You truly were something else!"

What happens when two middle-aged women, seasoned by time and life experience, escape their otherwise normal, if not predictable lives, and cruise the high seas in search of paradise? During their short adventure, they manage to solve a mystery bringing two unsuspecting families together, in a most surprising and unusual way. Set sail with Eve Gladwell in her amazing story, **The Floating Heirloom.**

THE FLOATING HEIRLOOM

Between the hedgerows— that is the way she had always thought of it— those straight, long, narrow country roads cutting through the Florida landscape. Those roads that box you in with thick vegetation that seems to loom over the road, as if ready to swallow you up and hold you captive along with so many other secrets being hidden in the miles of dense pines, Black Jack Oak with their shaggy moss beards and Palmetto Palms, spreading their fans in the tropical tangle. Humankind seems almost alien and unwanted in this primal lushness, but there it is, none the less, that long, straight ribbon of road piercing the jungle, and humanity moving up and down, in and out like ants, living life among the hedgerows.

Often the air is thick and pungent humming, buzzing, palpable with life. Evelyn Gladwell, otherwise known as Eve, smacks at the bite of a no-see-um as she worked in her garden. Plucking black and orange oleander caterpillars from her flowering bushes, she wished they had a respectable appetite to help with the microscopic demons swarming in the morning sun. Across a small expanse of lawn, she heard the ticking of her Rain Bird as it drenched the bright blue plumbago, azaleas, and dogwood that mark the perimeter of her garden, holding the forest at bay. *Tick, tick*— pregnant water droplets brought birds in to splash, preen and dance under the rainbow of cascading water. *Tick, tick, splash*— and still Mr. Whiskers does not move his sleek, feline, sun bathed self. His once vigilant squinted eye, now in quiet repose, is dreaming of birds from another day.

As Eve pulled off her more-than-worn garden gloves and tucks a roaming strand of gray hair behind her ear, she surveys her kingdom, her glorious patch of turf and smiles. She loved being out in the garden at this early hour when the sun yawns and stretches its rays across a big, blue sky to begin another day. The sweetness of the air and damp earth filled her with a sense of renewal and promise, a natural high she had come to expect and appreciate. Eve's roots were as strong and sustaining as the 100-year-old oaks that surrounded her modest home. She, like the oaks, had spread her seeds of heart, soul and life experience deep into the sandy loam of central Florida. It was truly home, all that she knew and loved. This unique landscape was comfort, security, peace and contentment. All created in her a sense of belonging.

Reveling in the thought of that first cup of coffee Eve had set to brewing earlier on her way through the kitchen, now drew her inside to pour a cup and to sit for a moments rest. Casper purred and curled around Eve's legs as she reached for her cream and sugar. Sipping at the fresh brew, she reached down for the meowing tabby and ruffled its fur. Now, one would have thought two cats plenty enough for care and company but they would be wrong. There were four other cats roaming, patrolling and lounging about; Ginger, who was spotted with multi colors, sported an alley cat look; Samantha, or Sam, was plump, long-haired and a soft solid gray; Harley, a neutered tom, was white with one black foot to match his one bad eye (too many turf battles in his past); and Muffin, who was somewhat timid, and still a kitten had brown and white markings. Yes, Eve had heard all the goofy jokes about old women living with too many cats to be regarded as sane or sensible, but it mattered little to her what others thought. One by one she rescued, or had been adopted by, her furry family and was perfectly content with their unconditional love and companionship.

Taking the steaming cup of coffee to her porch rocker, Eve settled in and moved with a gentle, rhythm, the creaking rocker keeping perfect time. Having been a widow for six years now and with three grown children dispersed here and there, Eve was content to enjoy the small, quiet, creature comforts. Sam jumped into her lap and playfully swatted at the strings of her peasant blouse, then kneaded herself into a spot on Eve's lap to be rocked to sleep. Closing her eyes, Eve felt the light, morning breeze brush her cheeks and whisper through the trees beyond her doorstep. Rocking and sipping at her coffee she thought, *I suppose there are many ways to live one's life.*

Our attitudes, experience and circumstance often nudge us down one road or another thought Eve. She had crossed paths with many other sojourners in her life and laughing with pleasure at the thoughts of some while trying to forget others. As she rocked and sipped her coffee this beautiful morning, Eve took time to reflect on her life and random images crowded her mind.

The exuberance she had experienced primarily in youth, seemed to exist between the parameters of great expectation and liberal doses of naiveté. The picture of turnips falling off a truck tickled her imagination.

Then there had been the challenging moments of uncertainty, where fear of the unknown had settled in, challenging all she thought she knew about herself. It was surprising what one could endure she thought with an uncanny grin.

For Eve, optimism was akin to her unwitting desire for survival. She had tenaciously latched onto the life force God had put within her. There had been surprising moments when she was full of an unquenchable excitement and bravado, a wellspring of hope, desire and possibility; for life was good and she felt blessed.

Then there had been those along her journey that had filled her life with love. Is it they who really understand and fully experience this magic, epic, adventure called life? Those whose hearts are filled with awe and gratitude each day with the wonder of it all? They are the ones who stand with outstretched arms willing to embrace their own humanity and that of others that season to taste the richness of our very existence?

Eve had known others who were stuck in one mindset or another and paid a dear price for their inability to budge But, what she now longed for, at the age of sixty-four, was to find contentment in her own skin and to distill wisdom from the lessons of her past, accepting her present life with all its blessings and limitations and to count it all good.

As she continued rocking and philosophizing, she detected a ring at her kitchen door. Disposing of Sam, she rounded the corner of her wraparound porch to find Happy Crenshaw at her back door, nervously ringing her hand as if agitated with great anticipation. Eve had seen her this way before. Happy was used to using Eve as a sounding board on all important issues, both foreign and domestic. Foreign would be anything Happy just couldn't understand, like why the Garden Club had to move the spring fundraising bazaar to the first of June instead of conforming to club rules that clearly dictated the third weekend in May. Domestic issues had mostly to do with Hubert, Happy's husband of forty-three years and their continual tug of war over who actually wore the pants in their family. One could only guess at the type of complaint of her mission this morning. With a sigh and a smile, Eve called to her friend who exhibited instant relief at the sight of her.

"Hello, Happy!" Eve called out, her coffee mug set aside on the window sill and arm extended for the usual hug. "Isn't it a perfect morning? You are out and about early," she continued as she opened the kitchen door and ushered her friend inside. "Would you like some coffee?" she inquired as she lifted the pot.

Once they had their mugs filled and were seated at the kitchen table, Happy looked straight into Eve's eyes and blurted out her exciting news.

"Eve, do you remember that horticultural contest I entered four months ago?" Eve motioned her acknowledgement.

"Well," she went on, wide eyed with exuberance, "I won! I won!

"You are joking," said Eve in a conspiratorial giggle, hands brought to her mouth in amazement. "Oh my word, I love it!" she shouted out. "So what is the prize, what have you won?" Eve enquired.

"Only a luscious seven-day cruise for two to a tropical paradise!" Happy shrieked, pulling a colored brochure from her purse. Happy went on to explain that the port of call was Bermuda, surrounded by beautiful, clear turquoise waters, sea breezes and thatched cabanas where one could lull about, strung up in a hammock and eat sumptuous food prepared by someone else until you literally explode.

"What's not to love?" said Eve as she sat back in her chair, smiling.

As the conversation drew on, Happy further explained that her darling Hubert, though proud of her success and good fortune at winning a prize, was not remotely interested in floating about the sea with a bunch of total strangers, trying to make small talk and kill time. A look of despair mixed with agitation washed her face.

"Will you come with me?" she pled as she hugged her mug for security. "Oh please say you will come!" Eve for once was truly dumbfounded and taken by surprise.

"I don't quite know what to say," Eve replied, truly stunned by the invitation.

Four weeks later, as the two middle-aged women bustled up the gangplank and onto the main promenade deck of the royal vessel *Oceana*, they poked at and smiled at one another, like two adolescents set free to explore the fair. Neither Happy nor Eve had ever sailed before except to Gilligan's Island with Ginger, Maryann, and the Skipper who were mostly marooned rather than negotiating the swells of the open sea. Such had been their exposure to exotica. But today, under the bright blue skies of the port of Miami, true adventure and excitement filled the air. With great anticipation, they waited along with their fellow passengers for their departure, when the anchor would be drawn and the fabulous, gleaming vessels bow would slice the deepening waters just beyond the port. Shouts of goodbye rang out, along with excited, waving hands, bidding farewell came from both the ship and dockside, where all shared in the thrilling moment when the ten-story, floating hotel budged from its moorings.

"Here we go!" shrieked Happy.

"Oh, I just can't believe it!" said Eve.

The first duty of all passengers of the Oceana, was to become familiar with the life-saving drill of evacuation, should the ship decide to take a turn downward instead of proceeding on as planned. Once all guests were gathered on deck, each person was handed an orange life vest and then the complicated instructions of adjustment were given: throw it over your head around your neck and tighten the belt. It was actually amusing to see how many people struggled with this amazing, simple, protocol. Eve and Happy performed like the two Girl Scouts they had been. The Life Vest badge would be theirs. After marching like orange penguins to their assigned launch boat locations, everyone was dismissed and told to explore their quarters and give the steward's office a ring if anything was needed.

As the two women made their way along the narrow corridors of C deck, C being short for "Celestial," they entered cabin 301C, a somewhat spacious accommodation by ship standards. The cabin possessed a small balcony with a spectacular view of the sky and sea, divided by an endless horizon. They found their luggage neatly stacked to one side near the door and crisp white linens folded on their beds in the shapes of birds, fans and sea creatures. Tucked inside their shell-shaped washcloths was a chocolaty, minty morsel that said, "Welcome home for the next few days." Eve and Happy threw their arms around each other and squealed with delight. Chocolate had never tasted so good.

Eve and Happy entered the dining room for the first call and to their astonishment, were seated at the Captain's table, a perk Happy had not anticipated. The table they were directed to was large and round with seating for twelve. It was set with creamy white linens, beautiful china and cut glassware, arranged in a pinwheel around a sumptuous, fresh-cut centerpiece all under a glistening chandelier. Such opulence was resplendent throughout the dining room.

Oh, and there he was just ahead of them in full regalia, the captain, a man in his 60s in formal, dress whites for evening dining. His brass was shining just like the sparkle in his bright, blue eyes. This striking man in uniform stood six feet tall, was slim and had a handsomely trimmed gray beard to match his thick thatch of hair, cut short and neatly combed. Captain Henry Jenkins was a fine looking fellow, with an even arrangement of manly features all tied together with a healthy tan and a charming broad smile that now greeted his guests this first evening at sea. With everyone seated, there was a clanking of glasses as the Captain lifted his goblet, poetically invoked comforting words concerning smooth sailing. The twelve diners smiled, greeting one another with an exchange of names, where they were from and what sort of work they were engaged in, if any. *What fun to meet new people, from many different places, all with their own story to tell*, thought Eve, smiling. She looked over the assembled and placed her napkin in her lap to commence the serving of the first course. It was just then that she noticed something interesting about the lady sitting directly across from her.

Miss Rochelle Hemings, an attractive if not voluptuous, young woman of twenty- nine, had introduced herself as a New Yorker, though having been born and raised in Madison, Wisconsin. She had fled her home town at the age of twenty- three to pursue an acting career in the Big Apple, but the apple apparently had a worm, for she struggled and failed to attract a top agency to represent her, and so had been relegated to random performances in off of Broadway, in what amounted to dank, small rooms in the basements of old hotels, but like all *ingénues*, the dream lived on.

The facts about her budding career as an actress, however, were not what had caught Eve's attention, interesting though they were. No, it was the diamond pendant, hung on a delicate gold chain around Miss Heming's slender, ivory neck that caught her eye. It had a beautiful spray of modest diamonds with a distinct, antique design. The mounting was shaped in a semi-circle with a larger stone that dangled in the middle of its lustrous crescent. It was a unique design she had only seen just once before, in a picture of her aunt Helen Marcum taken in the 1920s.

The family story was that Uncle Jim Marcum, as a young man, had worked for the railroad helping to develop passenger service to central and south Florida just as tourism to the state was beginning to boom. As a newlywed, he wanted to dazzle his young bride with a fabulous first anniversary gift she would always remember. He commissioned a jeweler in Miami to create a stunning design on a lucky horseshoe theme, a key ideal they would share as an excited young couple, full of the usual hopes and aspirations, rushing hand in hand into the future, and that extraordinary decade known as the Roaring Twenties.

Could there be two in existence? Eve pondered as she gazed at the sparkler. Aunt Helen's necklace had been custom designed just for her, to the specifications of an adoring husband. But, there it was or her name wasn't Evelyn Gladwell! As the evening progressed with courses of delectable food, laughter and chit-chat, Eve knew she must find a way to engage Miss Hemings in a conversation that would lead to the beautiful necklace and how it had been acquired. Perhaps she would see her in the powder room after dinner.

As the ladies politely excused themselves and made a mass exit to the LLA, Ladies Lounge Area, Eve fell into step behind the gaggle of talking women, while trying to keep an eye on Rochelle Hemings. At the paint and powder stage of the operation, Eve and Happy were positioned at the mirror and making repairs when Rochelle nestled herself right between them, lipstick in hand. Eve locked eyes with Rochelle in the mirror, flashing her a winning grin. Rochelle smiled back making some comment about the wonderful dinner they had just consumed and something about exploding. Eve and Happy gave each other a knowing glance. What's not to love! Eve then took a long, slow breath and turned to the subject at hand.

"I couldn't help noticing," Eve said, as she casually diddled with her hair, "your beautiful necklace, it has such an unusual mounting, where ever did you find something so unique?"

Rochelle gently caressed the stones at her throat with her fingertips and looked at Eve with appreciation for noticing their beauty and fine craftsmanship. Turning to face Eve, with a quizzical smile she said, "It's actually a family piece. I received it on my 21st birthday from my parents. I am the fourth generation to enjoy wearing it," and with that Rochelle turned and waved to Eve and Happy as she made her exit from the lounge.

Eve, stunned by this news, held on to the dressing table for support. Happy, perplexed by Eve's behavior, reached out for her friend's arm and asked if she was all right. Eve made her way to the nearest chair in the lounge and motioned for her friend to sit beside her. During the next few minutes Eve explained to Happy her interest in the necklace and her own family history with the piece.

"Do you really think it is the same one?" Happy asked, her voice filled with intrigue.

It was an original, custom design, Eve reminded her. "I will simply need to know more about Miss Heming's family to make a connection."

Their first night at sea turned out to be an interesting one to say the least. Now back in their room, Eve and Happy had wandered out onto their balcony to take in the warm sea breeze. Overhead hung a plethora of bright, twinkling stars in the midnight sky, again reminding Eve of the diamonds. Soon a discussion ensued about how to contact Miss Hemings and find out more about her family without seeming inquisitive to the point of embarrassment. How had a young woman from Wisconsin come to possess a lovely, antique pendant, loved by another in Florida so many years ago? Yes, this adventure to Bermuda had taken a new turn for Eve, but Happy was also drawn in by the mystery of it all and wondered if her penchant for crossword puzzles could help them connect the dots. They needed more information.

At the on-deck Café Royal, Eve and Happy munched on delectable, buttery warm croissants and hot Jamaican coffee for breakfast, while wondering what the day would bring. There were shops to explore, entertainments to see and later a dip in the pool would be grand. Eve looked around the classically designed café situated between enormous potted palms that punctuated the room. It was truly exotic and luscious. She observed many other patrons enjoying their food and conversations. Eve smiled about the wonderful time she was having when she noticed a slender woman in a bright, red sundress moving toward a table situated along the back wall of the café. The woman pulled out a chair and turned to look at a man and woman already seated there; it was Rochelle Hemings.

Eve nudged Happy and with a directing nod of the head they both looked at Rochelle.

"I wonder who she is sitting with?" asked Happy.

Rochelle made a comment to her companions and lightly touched the man's arm as she seated herself. All three laughed, smiling at one another. Eve explained to Happy that she mustn't lose this opportunity to speak with Miss Hemings or she would need to contrive another chance meeting. Eve was determined to satisfy her curiosity about the necklace.

Eve motioned to Happy and off they went. When they approached the table at the back of the room, Rochelle looked up and noticing them, she waved. Eve strode up to the table with her most engaging smile and bid Miss Hemings a chipper "Good Morning." Rochelle gave a friendly response then turned to her companions and proceeded to explain that these two ladies had dined with her at the Captain's table the night before and that she could only remember their first names: Eve for the mother of us all and Happy, that which we all wish to be. It was a little name game Rochelle played with herself to remind her of people's names. Rochelle then introduced her table companions.

"Eve, Happy, this is Irene and Harold Hemings, they are my parents."

"How delightful to meet you," said Eve with enthusiasm. "I know you are so proud to have such a beautiful and charming daughter." Mother and Father smiled in agreement.

"Mom," said Rochelle, "Eve was interested in our necklace. I wore it to dinner last night."

"Oh ,yes," said Irene, her warm, brown eyes expressing her fondness for the piece. Irene confirmed she had worn the pendant for years and now it was Rochelle's turn to enjoy it. Eve commented again on the unique, antique design, setting the stones in a dazzling display to catch the eye.

"And so they did," Irene retorted, "but that's a story for another day."

Eve's eyebrows rose in amazement as she said; "Irene, I would love to talk more with you about this necklace. There is a reason I am so interested in it." Irene, now intrigued, said they all had arranged to meet for a swim on E deck at 4:00 p.m. and if Eve and Happy hadn't other plans, were welcome to join them for refreshments and they could talk more then. And so it was agreed.

"Thank you for your invitation," said Eve. "We will see you at four."

That afternoon the pool area was a festive place, dotted with mini cabanas providing refreshment and shade where many had gathered. Others clustered about the pool's edge on lounge chairs, like so many lizards out soaking up the tropical sun. The Hemings were spotted by Eve, under a thatched roof at the leeward side of the deck already with drinks in hand; sunglasses positioned and snacks by their side. There was a Reggae band that tinked away in the background, adding to the joyful atmosphere.

Eve and Happy made their way to the Hemings' location where they exchanged friendly greetings and more chairs were pulled into the shade and more drinks were ordered as they got settled. After the usual small talk about the beautiful weather and the refreshing water, the conversation moved on to the subject of their meeting.

Eve began by saying, "Irene you indicated this morning that there was a story to be told about the necklace and it catching some one's eye. What did you mean by that?"

"What I meant by that," Irene said, "was that it had caught the eye of someone and they stole it."

"You are kidding" said Eve. "Tell us what happened."

Irene relaxed back in her chair, with elbows planted on its arms, she exercised her finger tips together in a spreading fan, her mode of concentration while she recalled the details.

"You see," she went on; "I received the necklace from my mother when I graduated from Duke University in North Carolina during the late 60s. While at school, I met Harold, she gave him a smiling glance, "and we fell in love and after graduation married".

Irene went on to explain that Harold was offered a job in Madison, Wisconsin, with an engineering firm that made steel trusses used for large super structures like skyscrapers and bridges. We moved to Madison and rented an apartment. We had been there only six months when it happened. We had gone to a large public gathering, a fundraiser for a local charity that Harold's company sponsored. I wore the necklace that night with a green chiffon dress I purchased especially for the occasion. As the evening progressed, I received a few compliments on my necklace. During our many conversations with various people, questions like, what is your name? Where do you work? And where do you live in the city," were freely discussed. That night was the last time I saw my necklace for the next three-and-a-half years.

Two days after the charity benefit, I came home in the late afternoon from a little part-time job I had, to discover the apartment had been robbed. Our TV, stereo, cameras and jewelry had all been stolen. We of course, called the police and made an inventory of what was missing.

From time to time that first year, we checked with the police, but to no avail. There had been a rash of break-ins, but no leads to the identity of the thieves. Three-and-a-half years after the necklace was taken, the police ran a sting operation on a male and female, suspects they thought may be part of a drug operation. One afternoon they followed the couple to their home in the suburbs. The raid on their house revealed a stockpile of drugs, lots of cash and various other stolen goods. As the police did a sweep of the residence, they discovered my necklace in a jewelry box on the dresser in the master bedroom. Evidently, the thief decided she wanted the necklace for herself and had no doubt been wearing it.

Eve was impressed with Irene's story. The lovely necklace could have been gone forever. What good fortune to have it recovered after all hope was lost. Life is often full of surprising twists and turns and this was surely one of them.

Irene now turned her gaze on Eve and said, "You mentioned earlier there was a particular reason you are so interested in the necklace, what is it?"

Eve, now feeling more comfortable with the Hemings, launched into her story about her Great Aunt Helen Marcum and her husband Jim. She told them her grandfather Eugene was the brother of Helen and her twin sister Suzanne. The Hemings were totally fascinated by this bit of information and looked at one another with sheer astonishment. Irene then shared that her mother Angela was the daughter of Suzanne who had been a Gladwell before her marriage to Eric Stevens. Stone silence fell over the group as each tried to grapple with this news.

Happy, believe it or not was the first to connect the dots and jumping from her seat and blurted out, "You are distant cousins, you are related, you belong to each other." There was another moment of silence, then first a giggle, then out and out laughter from them all. Eve clapping her hands for joy proclaimed, "This is so incredible, that we should have this chance meeting. I suppose fate has its own way."

For the next two hours, the Hemings and Eve Gladwell remained in a huddle under their thatched roofed cabana, filling in the blanks of their individual family histories for one another. There were minimal interruptions when the waiter occasionally inquired about the need for more food or drinks, and the lounge lizards made a mass migration from their pool side perch to the cooling waters with a splash. However, some interesting facts came to light as the group shared. For example, Great Aunt Helen died young in the 1930s from tuberculosis and how Uncle Jim struggled on through the Great Depression without the love of his life by his side. They had tried to have a baby but remained childless. As Helen lay dying in a sanatorium, she gave her twin sister Suzanne her necklace as a keepsake, a special gift, a token of remembrance to the sister she had loved.

Suzanne had met Eric Stevens at a dance in Jacksonville, Florida. They dated and eventually married and later had two sons and a daughter Angela, who was Irene's mom. Suzanne's husband Eric was a veterinarian, working in the newly established dairy industry in south Florida. He had been one of the early investors in the first state certified dairy in Miami, owned by Jimmy and Madie Ives.

Today there is a large boulevard, as you approach Miami from the north, sporting their name, Ives Dairy Road. Suzanne's daughter Angela, who would later become Irene's mother, was all of twenty and working the front desk of the Flagler Hotel in St. Augustine, Florida, a historically rich seaside resort; when Fredric Coleman, a young executive with Southern Bell, Florida's telephone company, walked to the desk and reached for the registry to sign in. It must have been that crooked, cheesy smile on his handsome face that made Angela notice him. Fred was in town for a conference and needed accommodations for a three-night stay. Over the course of those few days, the two shared casual conversations. A date for coffee was made the afternoon of Fred's departure that lasted well into dinner. With many shared interests and a love for the ocean, they began to correspond and date as their schedules permitted. It was at the beach one moonlit night that Fred proposed. With the answer to his question being yes, a grand reception was held at the Flagler ballroom and friends from far and wide were invited to share in the couple's joy. Angela received the keepsake necklace on her wedding day. It was the perfect complement to the stunning satin wedding gown she wore.

As the situation heated up in Europe, Fred felt duty bound to join the service and fight against the Nazi onslaught. By this time, Angela had given birth to Irene and a baby brother Rodney. Fred threw his hat in to train as an aviator, who would later duel with the Third Reich's ace pilots over the not-so-friendly skies of Germany. On his twenty-seventh bombing mission, Fred's plane was shot down over Kaiserslautern, the area where the huge Opal Works factory made tanks for the German Panzer Division. Unfortunately, Fred's body was never recovered. In the immediate years that followed, Angela honed her skills as a secretary and began working for a law firm, raising her two children on her own.

And so it had all been mapped out and explained, even to Happy's satisfaction. All the dots were connected and new alliances formed. As it was understood, Suzanne received the necklace from her dying sister Helen in the 1930s. Suzanne gave the necklace to her daughter Angela on her wedding day in the 40s. Angela then gave Irene the necklace when she graduated from college in the 60s. Irene gave the necklace to Rochelle on her 21st birthday in the 80s. How astounding that this precious, delicate antique had survived the transitioning years, even loss, and in the end was right where it belonged, around Rochelle Heming's neck.

The remainder of the cruise was a pure delight. The duty-free shops held enticements of every kind and description, food came and went in a sumptuous stream and yes, there was exploding, or at least a feeling that came close to it. Rochelle had to even admit on occasion how the lavish entertainment rivaled her beloved Broadway. Bermuda was all that had been hoped for. It was every bit the lush, balmy, tropical paradise featured in Happy's brochure. They had strolled and frolicked on its expansive, white beaches and been there at dusk, when the sky was a brilliant, crimson blaze and sea birds rode the waves for their evening catch. They toured villages, visited the bazaar and fruit markets, and ate native foods bought from street vendors. Happy even picked up a fine pair of hand-tooled leather sandals for a song. Throughout their travels, Eve and Happy were frequently in the company of the Hemings and found themselves together that last day of the cruise, as the Oceana pulled in to dock at Miami. Phone numbers, addresses and e-mails were exchanged. What a fabulous trip this had been. No one had imagined when the ship left port over a week ago that long-lost relatives would be found and a mystery solved. As Eve and Happy now neared the gangplank to disembark, hugs and kisses were freely given as Eve and the Hemings pledged to stay in touch through their joyful tears of new-found sentiment.

Hubert greeted the girls and stowed their luggage (that had grown considerably) into his old SUV.

"So how was it then?" he asked, as he navigated the parking lot and headed toward the freeway. Eve and Happy laughed as they rolled their eyes at one another.

"Oh I'll tell you all about it when we get home," said Happy. "It was quite a trip."

Hubert then glanced in his rearview mirror and shot Eve a mischievous grin, as she sat in the back seat.

He said, "Now how many cats did you tell me to feed while you were gone? I could only find ten."

Carried away by the music that was her passion, Sonya Riselman, a beautiful, young and talented cellist never dreamed of a life beyond the conservatory that was now her home. A chance meeting opens her heart and life to wonderful new opportunities and major tragedy. Read about her miraculous and tender journey in **The Cellist**.

THE CELLIST

$\mathcal{B}$ach's Suite No.1 in G Major was being delicately coaxed and romanced from Sonya's finely tuned Braga cello, as she purposefully bent into her bow and feverishly worked her fingers up and down the yielding strings. The sparse music room she worked in that cold winter afternoon resonated with an echoing rhythm, as rain tapped on the leaded windows and the sun offered only a modest light through the chilling downpour outside. With her eyes closed, she focused on the cords pulled low, then even lower until her heart was near breaking and she shuddered with ecstasy. Now swaying with the melody, she sailed off into her other world where the lush richness of classical music had lured her with such passion, that she could find no escape and so was taken captive, only to find release in the music itself that had now become her life.

Sonya Riselman wore her twenty-two years with a prodigious intensity that escaped most young women of her generation in the 1950s. Introduced to the world of music at the age of eight through the piano, she had found her soul in the cello by the age of fourteen and had earnestly dedicated her endeavors to becoming the finest cellist of her day. Opportunities to be involved with music had presented themselves early on and in rapid succession, as her prodigious talent came to be recognized by both her parents and delighted instructors. Young Sonya's life was literally lived out against a backdrop of the greatest composers who were ever inspired to write and their music played in her heart and mind with such clarity and precession as to leave her both physically and emotionally breathless at the end of a beautiful concerto. That God had seen fit to grace her with this wondrous gift she so loved, truly fulfill all of her wants and needs.

The San Francisco Conservatory of Music had accepted Sonya into its program some two years ago and she had exhibited remarkable progress under the tutelage of Inga Hoffelmeyer, an excellent instructor who had received her own musical education from the Berlin Philharmonic during the turbulent 1940s, then had immigrated to the United States at the conclusion of the war. The San Francisco Conservatory, being the only top-rated music school in the western United States was a natural pick for Sonya, who had been born and raised in Sacramento, California, and had visited the dazzling City by the Bay on many occasions in her youth. Sonya was attracted to the school for many reasons, aside from her main concerns,which were its top rating, wonderful strings department and convenient student housing. The other reasons had more to do with San Francisco itself. The vibrant social life of the city offered so many amenities to living a cultured life steeped in the arts; one only had to ask, what shall we do next? There were also many opportunities for small ensemble groups to find work, plying their trade and making useful connections that would serve them well later on. Yes, it was an idyllic, inspiring environment for a young artist seeking her way.

Now completed with her rehearsal, Sonya moved her nimble body from the cushioned seat where she sat and began to pack away her music and instrument to protect them from the rain as she prepared to make a mad dash across campus to her student quarters. As she clicked the buckles closed on her cello case, the music room door swung open and in walked Inga, rubbing her long, white fingers while complaining about the rain and cold. Sonya herself had hoped the rain would have let up by now, but often when weather moved into the bay, it sat there for a day or two, then of course there was always the fog.

Inga stood near the window now and while removing her glasses to rest her eyes, inquired as to how the practice session had gone that day. She noted the double forte in the second measure of the third movement called for vigorous energy.

Sonya laughed and told Inga she had given it a real workout. They smiled at one another and Inga said, "That's my girl!"

Sonya commented that the Elgar Cello Concerto had been an exciting challenge at first, but now she just loved and looked forward to the breathtaking jumps as the music moved from octave to octave, then rushes in with a series of half notes. Inga grinned, and said she felt this piece of music had been a watershed moment in classical music history, that really represented the breadth and depth of what the wonderful cello is capable of.

Inga then went on to remind Sonya that the back entrance to the staging area for the Kessler Museum was actually on the left side of the building and to arrive early Saturday night allowing plenty of time for set-up. The gala fundraiser was a wonderful event, one of the more prestigious affairs held in the city each year. All the movers and shakers would be there dressed to the nines, with their checks already written. These same donors were the very people who so generously supported the conservatory, so it was a given that the music school would contribute to this lavish affair.

Early that Saturday evening as Sonya added her single strand of cultured pearls to her black, taffeta floor-length gown, she reached for her comb one last time for a final go at her thick, lustrous, auburn hair that fell in deep waves and curls to her slight shoulders. Her fair porcelain skin was set a dazzle by her two startling, luminous blue eyes that now glanced anxiously back at her from the mirror as she made her final appraisal. Next, grabbing he wool coat, she also collected her cello that stood near the door. The school always provided transportation to concert venues, so as she approached the waiting van, Fred Danielson one of the conservatory's drivers, reached for Sonya's cello and happily helped her aboard.

The museum soon resonated with the clatter of music stands being put in place and the clamor of instruments being finely tuned for the work at hand. This was always an exciting time for the young artists, as they waited in anticipation for the opening moments of their program of classical favorites, played for an enthusiastic, appreciative audience. This evening's offering would begin with Vivaldi's Concerto No.10 in B Flat, then move on to Bach's Air on G String, Handle's Largo, and Pachelbel's Canon. The evening would conclude with the breathtakingly beautiful Elgar Cello Concerto that always brought audiences to their feet in rousing approval. Now taking their seats for the final call, the musicians made quick, last minute adjustments to their seating and music stands as the conductor hushed them into silence and full attention. Then, with one grand swoop of the maestro's wand, the poised, silent instruments were quickly awakened and passionately thrust into the stirring notes of the first movement.

It was indeed a magical night with the museum aglow in ambient light, champagne flowing from ornate, crystal fountains that were garnished with pale, cream colored orchids and exotic passion flowers; and yes, the fabulous music played with passion and grace. It all seemed to underscore what Beethoven supposedly once said to a friend, "That when God whispers in man's ear the result is music and that musicians move with the spirit of God to learn his language and then share it with the world." The richness of this interpretation had been manifested brilliantly during the largo segment of the program, as the first movement morphed into the second with cello pulled low held earthbound, while other strings soared heavenward suspended, playing to the rapturously expressive nature of the piece that always held the audience spellbound. The entire evening had been an absolute triumph in every way and Sonya found herself once again amazed to have experienced such a moment as this.

As the rich, if not famous, convened that evening, now filed out the front doors of the museum to waiting cars and taxies, the orchestra members gathered their belongings and bantered back and forth about the success and splendor of the evening. The first seat violinist, Bertram Hathaway, nicknamed Bird by his friends, flashed a winning glance Sonya's way and commented on her stellar performance that night, to which she curtsied and grinned back her thank you. For the past three months Bert had been warming to the idea of asking Sonya for coffee or dinner but had so far fought the urge until this very moment. Reaching for his long black coat and tugging on its sleeves, he casually asked Sonya if she had ever been to the Café Devinci on Market Street, a known haven for artists and musicians. She admitted having heard of it but never having been there. Bert said a few students from the orchestra had decided to stop by there that night and he wondered if she might like to join them. Sonya looked him over for a brief moment, as he stood there tall and handsome before her and thought, *Why not, it might be a great way to end a wonderful evening.*

As they strolled up Market Street, the night mist swirled down the concrete canyons of sky scrapers, fog horns could be heard out in the bay and the occasional rattle and bell of a cable car echoed in the distance. Opening the door to the café for Sonya, Bert then called out and waved to friends seated near the bar. There was Jimmy Turner, a wonderful viola player who was built like a wrestler, short and stock with a thick neck and broad shoulders; Erich Andrews, a base player sporting an impish grin and a pencil-thin mustache that danced up and down on his face when he spoke, and Margaret Salvo, a plain looking, serious, woman who was a brilliant pianist. The threesome, with drinks in hand, waved back at Bert and pushed to make room. Sonya recognized these students from their comings and goings but had never had an occasion to meet them until now. Bert happily made introductions, adding funny little quips about his friends and their musical resumes. Through laughter and the common thread of music, a new bond was formed and another round of drinks order.

The café was jammed that night and some slow bluesy music was being belted out in the back corner of the club by a beautiful, black woman in a tight-fitting, red satin gown. Her name was Lena Horne and she sang with soul and passion, holding the smoke-filled room captive with each evocative phrase. She was being accompanied by a black man on the piano that played every note to fit Lina like a glove, pulling the passionate lyrics from her lips, while piercing her heart with his sultry melody. As a small table was made available, the group resettled and focused in on the dreamy music.

As fate could have predicted, over the next several months, Sonya enjoyed many fun-filled opportunities to be with her newfound friends. Through on campus concerts and cavorting into the city, the merry five were filled with the invincible bravado and optimism of youth, along with their unstoppable zeal for their music. They were eventually led to form a piano and string ensemble and during off hours from the conservatory, they played expensive tea rooms, restaurants and many of the opulent homes poised as the crowning jewels of the city at the top of "Knob Hill." All the while however, other strings were being pulled by two hearts that had inadvertently fallen in love. Sonya and Bert found their shared drive and ambition for their music only served to heighten the passion of their budding love and desire for one another.

Six months after their declared feelings for each another, Bert moved off campus and took a small bungalow in the Mission District of the city, among the work-a-day people, the palpable energizers of civic life in the city. The butchers, the bakers, the candlestick makers were the new neighbors that graced his life with an earthy, rampant kaleidoscope of color and flavor he found exciting and inspiring. As

Sonya and Bert spent more time alone together, their thoughts turned to the immediate future and matters of graduation, with the completion of their studies coming to a close. Then, there would be the need to locate viable employment that would secure their futures in music. There was also their growing desire to be married and perhaps carry their careers forward as a dynamic duo with their zinging strings of violin and cello. There had been offers from others to help catapult the couple into this next phase of their lives, so now was the time to make some serious considerations.

It was on a rainy Thursday afternoon, in the bar at the Regency Hotel on Claremont Street, where Bert assembled his closest friends and produced a diamond ring that was scandalous in its sheer size and brilliant, dazzling cut. As he moved his arm around Sonya's waist and pulled her close, he pronounced to his companions that this ring was only as exquisite as the woman wearing it, hopefully for the rest of her life and the couple kissed while tears of joy welled up in Sonya's eyes. Shortly after, they were escorted into a beautifully appointed, private dining room where the engagement party inquired as to the wedding date. They were told that Sonya's parents wanted her to come home to Sacramento, her childhood church, family and friends to celebrate the nuptial. A date two months in advance had been selected, the fifteenth of May, when the blush of spring would grace the surrounding hillsides with a profusion of sweetness and blooming foliage. Sonya thought of being the quintessential spring bride in all her splendor.

As the wedding day approached and final arrangements were being etched in granite, Sonya could hardly believe that in one short week she would be Mrs. Bertram Hathaway, a married woman with a whole new exciting life ahead of her. Sonya left Bert, waving goodbye at the San Francisco Airport as she boarded her plane to Sacramento, home, where she would remain cloistered with the love and attention of her two doting parents until the big day. Bert stood at the railing and watched as Sonya disappeared into the stream of people filing through the door of the plane. His emotions were stirred with a sense of gratitude as he considered just how blessed he was to have the love and affection of such an extraordinary, beautiful woman. His only desire at that moment was to be the trustworthy guardian of her heart.

While Bert departed the gate and headed back to the main terminal, he grinned to himself as he thought about the honeymoon they had planned. They would first fly to New York City and spend a couple of days seeing the sights, then head for Rome, Italy. They planned to tour Rome, Florence, and Venice for the next fourteen days, seeing the art, attending the theater and would end their honeymoon in Florence at the Auditorium al Duomo, where they would experience in concert, two of their favorite Italian composers, Puccini and Vivaldi in the splendor of their native land. When Bert reached his car, he fished around in his pocket for his keys and grinned again in anticipation of the weeks to come.

While traveling away from the airport along the beltway that circled the city, Bert picked up on the noise of emergency sirens and noticed smoke billowing skyward from the direction of his home in the district. Taking his usual exit off the expressway, he found his neighborhood street jammed with spectators and traffic, as police frantically held people at bay and motioned rescue vehicles into place. Leaving his car in the long line of stalled traffic, he lit out on foot to get a closer look at what was happening. To his total shock and horror, he discovered that the section of row houses his own bungalow was attached to was ablaze in soaring flames. Bert panicked as he realized that his beloved Stradivarius violin was lying unprotected, out of its case on a table in his small parlor where he had practiced that morning. He had possessed that wonderful instrument for ten years and considered it to be another arm reflecting his soul at the center of his being. Dodging busy fireman, he ran frantically around the end of one of the apartments and scurried through an alley that led to a rear entrance of his bungalow. Pulling his jacket up over his head, he barged through his kitchen door and immediately began choking on the toxic, thick smoke that filled the room. Bright orange flames licked the walls of the hallway that led to the parlor and his violin. Now crouching on all fours, Bert began to crawl forward, gasping for every breath as he made his slow approach to the parlor. Through his stinging, burning eyes that now smarted with tears, he spotted the violin, reached out and grasped it tightly with both hands. Clutching it to his chest, he tried to retrace his way back to the kitchen but the flames had grown so intense he could barely move. Then, as he inched forward a couple of feet, he heard a fireman barking orders to others as they made for the back door and broke windows to shoot water inside. As Bert called out to them and made one last heroic effort to drag himself toward the door, a flaming ceiling beam wrapped in melting insulation fell on top of him, pinning him to the kitchen floor with his violin tucked under him. As he screamed out in agony, his last rational thought was, "I am going to die!"

The sheer pain and torture of the days that immediately followed came and went initially in a slow succession of suffering, fear, and uncertainty for this young couple who were finally ready to launch their lives together. All of that now appeared to have been viciously snatched away through a circumstance so hideous and unforeseen as to not be believed. How could something like this have happen? It was so incomprehensible that a situation as mundane as an unattended pan of sautéing onions could escalate into a four-alarm fire that would ultimately consume six apartments and disfigure one man nearly to the point of death. The courageous human spirit is often a surprising and amazing thing when pushed up against all odds, and through the grace of God, this ultimately proved to be the case with Bert.

When Sonya heard the news, she immediately flew back to San Francisco, so relieved to know her dear Bert was still alive, though badly burned for the rescue efforts of his beloved violin. Rushing into his hospital room, she collapsed bedside in a puddle of tears as she saw Bert lying in bed wrapped like a mummy. Even the left side of his handsome, manly, face was shrouded with gauze that was taped to his skull. But it was Bert, with a fractured back and burns over forty percent of his body, that first tried to reach out with a weak smile to comfort his sweet bride-to-be.

Over the next several months, Bert underwent six skin grafting operations and extensive therapy for his back. It was a time that required tremendous patience, faith, and courage; yet through it all, Bert and Sonya pulled together, absolutely unwilling to give up on life and all they had planned for their future. The foundation of their abiding love and underlying deep friendship proved more enduring than the superficial scaring of Bert's body and was an indestructible force in helping him heal and regain an optimistic view moving forward. The man at his core had not changed. He was still the same smart, witty, wise, and loving individual he had always been, the very man Sonya had fallen in love with. Ultimately the plastic surgery on the left side of his face had a good result and his hands and fingers though still scared, were mending nicely with an ever-increasing nimbleness and flexibility. His dream of course, was to one day pick up his violin again, the very violin that miraculously had sustained a lot less damage than he had. When Bert and his instrument were salvaged from the charred ruins of his bungalow, the only problem detected with the violin was a fine hair line crack running the length of its hollowed core. Luckily, there had been an artisan in the city who was able to restore it to near perfection.

Finally dismissed from the hospital and ensconced in a new apartment on Powel Street, wedding plans were being revived with all the excitement and affections as the first time. After their European honeymoon, they would live at the Powel Street location, while continuing to play dates with the ensemble group and auditioning for more permanent work as it became available. One evening while resting in one another's arms on the balcony, looking out over the spectacular, glittering city of Venice, they concluded that they were two of the luckiest people alive and their hearts were filled with love and gratitude. Even though they didn't understand why people sometimes suffer tragedy in life, they had come to realize that you always have a choice as to what you will do with those times. Love, compassion and determination can be transforming, literally make all things new again for the brave heart, for where there is life there is always hope.

A Postscript:

In the years that followed their tumultuous beginning, Sonya and Bert's life settled into a natural rhythm that presented them with immense joy and opportunities to grow and flourish musically. Their personal life together had been enriched and blessed by the birth of their three children, Erich, Melanie and Stephen; and as one might have suspected each was ingrained with a love for music at an early age and given every opportunity to mine any musical talent they might possess. Erich developed a love for progressive jazz and took up the saxophone, while Melanie had a love for strings like her parents and so became a harpist. Stephen had been given a drum kit early on to help harness his boyish energy but eventually laid it aside to pursue other interests in sports.

By the early 1970s the couple with three small children in tow moved to Cleveland, Ohio, to pursue their professional careers and cultivate new opportunities to expand their influence in that musical community. The Cleveland Philharmonic Orchestra was going through a major transition and was reorganizing their strings department. As it turned out, both Bert and Sonya found a new home in the orchestra of sixty musicians who normally played six major concerts per year in the greater Ohio area when not on tour. These concerts were kept at a minimal cost to ticket holders in hopes of engendering more support and interest in music among its citizens.

Oberlin College had been another dream come true for the family. Not only was it near Cleveland in a beautiful, rural setting but its conservatory of music was considered one of the top music schools in the country, right next to Julliard. Not only did Erich and Melanie take advantage of this wonderful musical environment, but Bert and Sonya also had been given invitations to teach as visiting adjunct professors in the basics of ensemble repertory music. What a God-given blessing it was to be at the top of their game professionally and also be given access to the future of music through young eager musicians that would one day take their place. It was by divine order that Sonya and Bert had followed their passion and ultimately been led to each other and into a life overflowing with purpose, optimism and the exquisite, timeless gift of beautiful music.

Never die with your music inside you, whatever that music might be!

Just at the moment when time and circumstance are perfectly aligned in a sublime sweetness, almost incomprehensibly, fate steps into the breach between reality and perception, changing two lives forever. In one devastating instant, two perfect strangers; Robin Walker and Gary Owens are caught in the unrelenting jaws of the unforeseen and struggle against all odds to survive in **Here and Beyond.**

HERE AND BEYOND

$\mathcal{A}$s she drove across the long ribbon of bridge traversing Tampa Bay, the sky and water were a dazzling blue and the hot sun climbed its way high into the sky. The power of her sleek silver BMW sports car added to the exhilaration she felt as she sped along; the wind brushing her face, her short tresses fluffed by the breeze. Life was good and full of promise. Robin Walker smiled at herself in the rearview mirror as she glanced up to change lanes, while the mellow tones of her favorite jazz station filled the air and she tapped out the rhythmic beat with her fingertips on the steering wheel. The total freedom and joy she felt at this moment was intoxicating, something her limited years of experience lead her to believe could go on forever. And so she glided down the highway on this glorious, beautiful Florida morning ever closer to her ultimate destiny than one could have guessed or predicted, but isn't that the way of life?

Robin, having been engrained with a strong work ethic by her mother and a love for math by her father, had carried those attributes to the University of North Florida where she graduated top of her class with a degree in Economics and Business Administration. She then went on to secure a top job with a leading financial institution in Tampa, where she now worked as a financial strategist. Given the keys to the executive wash room and a six-figure salary, she had successfully negotiated the treacherous corporate waters and proved her worth to the firm. Now two years later, she was no longer considered the new kid on the block as she sat in her corner office on the twelfth floor at the age of twenty-nine, fully engaged in building the career she had only dreamt of during her college years.

Robin was looking forward to the weekend at St. Pete Beach with friends, a good chance to decompress from a hectic work schedule and the large project that had consumed her for weeks. Having moved over the bridge, she now took the Twenty-Second Avenue exit from the freeway where she would cut across town and head north a short distance up the Gulf Coast to the bungalow she and her friends rented for the weekend. How she longed to just lie in the sun and let her mind wander and later enjoy the salted rim of a frozen margarita, as she tossed a nice, fresh salad with juicy, red tomatoes and ripe avocado while shrimp kabobs sizzled on the grill. Yes, this was a perfect day in a perfect life and she was determined to make the most of it.

First in line at the stoplight at Twenty-Second Avenue and Thirty-Fourth Street, she smiled again and reached for the hot pink sun visor that sat in the seat next to her. Pushing it over her temples, she adjusting the brim. Noticing the light had turned green, she quickly shifted the car from first to second gear and entered the intersection. That was the last thing she remembered. What was left of her small car had spun around three consecutive revolutions and then jumped the curb wrapping itself around a light pole. The stunning impact of an oncoming vehicle at an accelerated speed, had not only made Robin and her car unrecognizable, but had done considerable damage to the other car as well, a white mid-size SUV and the man driving it. Now with metal and glass strewn over the entire intersection, some who had been nearby in traffic, jumped from their cars, two with their cell phones in hand making calls and taking pictures. The same bright, blue sky that had existed just moments before, when all was right with the world, now presided over the carnage below. In just a second, fate had stepped in and changed two lives forever.

Robin could barely be seen in the tangle of crushed metal that encircled her body, holding her in a vice grip. The entire frame of her car was nearly bent in half. Soon the scream of emergency sirens could be heard as onlookers gasped in horror, one or two rushing forward to check for signs of life. Smoke rose from both vehicles, the threat of fire loomed because of spilt fuel; fumes now permeated the air. First to respond was the fire department whose personnel jumped from their trucks and dashed to each car. Meanwhile, the police had arrived and began crowd control as they directed the ambulance through the mass of people now congregated on each corner of the intersection. The first help to reach Robin's car was Jimmy Jackson, a fireman who immediately dealt with a man whom had been in traffic right behind Robin's car and had seen the entire incident play out before his eyes. He paced up and down beside the wreckage wringing his hands as he tried to describe to Jimmy just how the wreck happened, it was all so fast!

Jimmy gently handed the man off to a nearby police officer and began the painstaking task of looking for Robin's body and any sign that she had survived impact. A corner of her hot pink visor was spotted first, and then an audible groan caught Jimmy's attention. Here was a place to start. As the scene was secured, the police began their investigation, taking statements and looking at cell phone pictures of the site. The EMT worked in tandem with fire rescue agents in caring for the drivers of both cars while the extraction process moved forward under the direction of the fire department.

Hanging at the end of a delicate thread of fate, a young life now dangled precariously in the balance, on the very threshold of mortality; a shadowland ill-defined, constrained by the mere whisper of a breath, barely perceptible. Robin's body, after what seemed like forever, had finally been pulled from the crumpled mass that was her pride and joy, and tenderly placed on a gurney, then rushed to a nearby St. Petersburg Hospital. Her vital signs were elusive like the flight of a butterfly, fluttering, hovering, able to fly away and be gone at any moment. As her cut, bruised, and broken body was rushed to the ER, her frail figure was already shrouded in several splints, IV tubes and an oxygen mask. The carefree dream of warm sand between her toes and the rush of waves as they lapped the shore now seemed a far-off illusion that lacked context or meaning. Where she was, and what had happened was a mystery. She floated in and out of consciousness, caught in a limbo devoid of time and space, a dimension known only to those who stand before the veil of eternity.

Gary Owens had a very bad headache, not unlike many he had lately. He knew the excessive drinking he had been doing alone each night was not the answer to the problems he faced, but sadly now it had become a new habit, his evening companion now that Sheryl, his wife of six years, had walked out on him and their marriage she claimed had become dull and stifling. Gary was the last one to realize how unhappy

Sheryl really was. He thought they were doing just fine. Over the past two years he turned his mechanical aptitude into a solid business of his own. He learned about the heat and air trade from his Uncle Ted who hired him as a helper when he was just finishing high school. Now a few short years later, he and his partner Jack Dawson had developed a solid base of residential clients and were beginning to work a few lucrative commercial contracts. He even felt confident enough to put a down payment on a modest home on a comfortable, tree-lined street where other young couples were settling in to raise their families. Gary didn't realize that dedication, hard work and setting goals for the future made him dull and stifling; he thought he was stepping up, doing what a man should do, but it wasn't enough.

Once again he took his broken heart and throbbing head in search of coffee and Excedrin; then perhaps a shower and a shave would help him feel human again. Later in the morning, dressed and with his oversized travel mug in hand, he decided to take advantage of a little free time over the weekend to check a job site they were going to begin working on Monday. The Carlyle Company out of Denver was building a new facility in Tampa as part of their national expansion campaign and Gary had landed the job, one that could take his own business to a new level.

Gary grabbed a notebook and pen from the kitchen counter, clipped his tape measure on his belt and picked up his keys. Settling in behind the wheel of his white SUV, he placed his mug in the cup holder, adjusted the windshield visor, and reached for his sunglasses to combat the morning light that assaulted his eyes and aching head. He left his cell phone in the car overnight and now checked to see if it needed charging. His neighborhood street was fairly quiet this morning. There were two kids on bikes moving down the sidewalk with an Airedale puppy in hot pursuit and a man retrieving his newspaper from his mailbox. *Life has a way of moving on with or without you*, Gary thought, as he rounded the corner and turned on to Twenty-Second Avenue.

Just as Gary completed his turn, his cell phone rang and he reached to pick it up. It was Sheryl in a curt and agitated voice. She began ranting that he had agreed to put money into her checking account until a legal settlement could be worked out, and had not done that, and why hadn't he picked up the used dresser from her girlfriend's garage that she needed for her new apartment. With his head pounding and the angry exchange with Sheryl becoming a shouting match, Gary decided to try and beat the light up ahead that had already turned yellow. Snarling into the phone he pressed down on the gas and charged through the intersection.

What he now felt was far removed from the mere headache and stress he experienced moments ago. His SUV stood silent and skewed in the middle of the intersection, the offending cell phone now thrown to the floor squawked on in spurts.

"Are you there, Gary?" A pause and then, "For Pete's sake, speak up I can't hear you."

Numb and startled, Gary noticed someone at his window looking in at him, asking if he was all right, but he could not concentrate on the words enough to formulate an adequate answer. Smoke rose from the front grill of his car as he choked and tried to move, but was unable. He had no recollection of the silver sports car darting out from under the light at Thirty-Fourth Street. He had been otherwise engaged, and even the reality of this moment eluded him as he slumped in his seat and passed out.

Hours later, emerging from the darkened shelter of his mind into the half-light of his hospital room, Gary Owens opened his eyes again for the first time since the accident. He had been placed in room 357 of the trauma ward on Saturday shortly after noon; it was now 5:30 a.m. on Sunday morning. Gary made an attempt to focus and survey his surroundings, but he felt lost in a fog induced by his injuries and the drugs he had been given. As he made a feeble gesture to move, he was assaulted with searing pain that shot through his body. He discovered he was tethered to his bed with an IV tube and a splinted arm and leg on his left side, all wrapped up like a mummy. Laying back on his pillow he disciplined his mind to think, to remember what had happened to him. He now slowly came to the realization he had been in his car, and yes, there had been the call from Sheryl. *There must have been an accident*, he thought. *Was there another car involved?* Oh no, he just couldn't remember another car, but there must have been one. As twilight played at his window, nurse Meg Stewart entered his room and smiled to see Gary's eyes open as she wheeled her cart of monitoring equipment alongside his bed.

"Welcome back to the world," she said in a warm, cheery voice as she inquired about his pain level, and replaced his empty IV bag with a new one. Gary looked at Meg with pleading eyes hoping she could fill in the blanks of his spotty recollection. She informed him he had been received in the ER yesterday shortly after noon, having been in an accident across town. There had indeed been another vehicle involved and that driver had been brought in as well. She had no other details relative to the other driver's identity or condition, and said that Dr. Morrison, who had taken care of Gary, would be doing rounds soon and would have more information concerning the accident, his injuries and what to expect in the weeks ahead. With one more sympathetic smile and a wish for his speedy recovery she was out of the room and down the hall to see her next patient.

Staring at the ceiling as if it could reveal the secrets of his recent past, Gary agonized over his own demise and could only wonder what had become of the other person involved in the accident. God help him, what was he going to do now. Still unclear as to the extent of his own injuries, he now worried about the new project he had to begin in the morning. He would need to get word to his partner Jack that he'd probably be out of commission for a while and that Jack would need to be on site with the crew in the morning. Then there were the regular calls that would need to be dealt with. This unforeseen complication into his already stress-filled life was an overwhelming intrusion he didn't need. As tears now glistened in his eyes, he remembered he couldn't even lean on Sheryl for any emotional or physical support, for the bridges between them were now burnt and lay in the smoldering ashes of their last conversation. Suddenly he felt adrift in a sea of depression and uncertainty with no anchor in sight, so he closed his eyes again, against a world he hadn't the strength or energy to cope with and sailed off into a fitful sleep.

Robin Walker underwent eleven hours of intense surgery to repair the extensive damage done to her vital organs and spinal cord, while doctors fought to control her massive bleeding. On three separate occasions they thought they had lost her, but she hung on, making it through the delicate procedures to sustain her life, but what of that life, so altered from the one she had been living just hours before. Robin had been placed in a special unit of the ICU where a full time RN attended her, checking and adjusting the life support systems that now sustained her. Robin's spirit clung tenuously to her motionless body, caught deep in the phantom realm of coma, drifting, floating between two worlds unrecognizable, suspended and held captive beyond the reaches of her own reality.

Robin's mother and father anxiously consulted with the two

surgeons that operated on their only child. Having been filled in by the police as to the accident itself, they now dealt with the anguish of uncertainty concerning their daughter's life that seemed tenuous at best. Doctors Richardson and Elders tried to compassionately explain all they had done in layman's terms, highlighting their main concern of probable paralysis, should Robin emerge from her comatose state and regain a reliable stage of stability. The very thought of their young, intelligent, vivacious daughter surviving this hideous accident only to be a paraplegic the rest of her life made Mrs. Walker shudder and crumple to her knees and she was led to a nearby chair.

Long silent days, except for the bleeps and flashing lights of monitors, passed into even longer nights of bedside vigils kept by family and loved ones, who by the sheer will of their presence, refused to let Robin slip away, unnoticed. They attempted to restrain her flight with their tears and their pleading, holding her limp hand in their own, sharing a life force transmittable only by love and longing. The days slipped into weeks and the torturous silence remained, taunting those held in their unabated grief.

Gary Owens was soon to be released from the rehabilitation center where he had spent the last several weeks convalescing and doing therapy on the arm and leg that had been so severely fractured. A steel rod attached to a plate with screws now held his left arm to his shoulder, just part of the permanent hardware holding him together that remained tender and sore and would be for the weeks ahead. The wheelchair he sat in had become part of his physicality and the only means by which he got around, his leg elevated most of the time. Life as he knew it had come to a screeching halt; his own personal pain a precursor for what he had come to fill, as he learned from the police, the full ramifications of his impetuous run through the yellow light at the corner of Twenty-Second Avenue and Thirty-Fourth Street. The awful truth of an innocent victim now lying in a coma crushed his soul and filled him with an unbearable gilt and remorse. Devastated and bewildered, he repeatedly damned himself for what had happened to Robin Walker. He felt an ever increasing need to visit her and see firsthand the reality of his misdeed. He had to put a face with the emotional pain he felt, then perhaps he could begin to cope with the entire situation, to see if there was any way to help undo the damage he'd done, an attempt to make things right. He had to try.

Jack Dawson pushed Gary in his wheelchair down the sterile, quiet corridors of the hospital while arguing the merits of his decision to visit Robin. Jack had stepped in after the accident and taken over full management of their operations and had proved himself to be a loyal a friend and partner. Over time, the two men had bonded with a brotherly kind of camaraderie and now Jack's only desire was to see his friend be well and happy again and of course back at work. He remained skeptical that seeing Robin Walker in her diminished state would promote a healthier perspective for Gary rather than drive him into deeper despair. Upon reaching Robin's room, Gary took a deep breath and asked Jack to wait for him as he pushed himself inside her room, positioning his chair beside her bed. Fortunately, those usually posted at her side this time of the day had taken a break leaving Robin alone for a few moments.

Gary sat beside Robin almost transfixed, hardly able to blink as he stared at her fragile body, pale, gentle face and shallow breath. She was a young woman, petite with a crown of short-cropped golden hair in a pixie cut that softened the features of her angular face. The thought that she would remain suspended, fixed in time, never again to talk or laugh and pursue her ambitions was hard to imagine. She had her whole life ahead of her, yet there she was.

"I have put her here," Gary mumbled to himself. He leaned over to rest his hands and chin on her bed rail, his sad eyes smarting from the tears forming now, as he continued to stare at her wondering what she would have been doing today if the accident hadn't happened. The remorse he felt at seeing her was almost suffocating, as he strained to maintain some degree of composure. Momentarily, he bowed his head in despair, pleading to God for help. His mind wandered through a maze of thoughts and emotions, when he heard a sigh that startled him, bringing him back into the moment. Gary looked at Robin with a flood of anxiety, and then it happened. With another slight moan Robin moved her head to the right and then opened her eyes. For a few short seconds, their eyes locked and the poignancy of that moment was virtually palpable. Robin Walker reentered the temporal world of her existence to find a stranger with a tear-streaked face staring at her from her bedside. The man, who ironically had destroyed her tender young life, was the first person to greet her as she reemerged from her cocoon of darkness back into the light of life.

Gary instantly, without thinking, reached out for Robin's hand, as a gentle smile lifted his face. At that same moment Robin's parents entered her room. Puzzled by Gary's presence they quickly moved to their daughter's bedside. The next thing to be heard was the resounding sobs of joy and relief as a rushed call was made to the nurses' station. Both parents began speaking at once to their only daughter whom they thought might be lost to them forever. In the excitement of the moment, Gary quietly withdrew from the room, gliding down the hall and out of sight, his presence now an afterthought, weighed against the miracle that had just happened. All attention was now focused on Robin and what could be done to sustain her awareness and nudge her forward toward some kind of recovery.

Gary grasped for words to adequately describe to his friend Jack, the electrifying moment when Robin first opened her eyes, while they drove from the hospital parking lot now lit by lamps with the onset of dusk. Gary's excitement was generated by a heart filled with gratitude, that Robin might actually have a fighting chance for some sort of recovery and that all was not lost. Over the weeks since he had become aware of her condition, he had prayed for her continually, bargaining with God for her life. He promised to put his own house in order. He promised to do all he could to make things better for Robin, whatever it took and he especially vowed to never take life for granted again, such a precious commodity that could be lost in a moment, squandered and gone. The fact that he had been with Robin at the very moment of her awakening was to him a sign of redemption and grace that would mark his life from that day forward.

Robin Walker's life had begun anew, like a flower that at first finds itself nothing more than a small bud of promise, then little by little grows, its fragile petals begin to unfurl ultimately exposing the fullness of its glory. Its core thrusting forward and exposed, it receives all that heaven intended it to be. Within the human soul, such refinements take many varied forms. Fears and vulnerabilities laid bare are often the very tools used to hone the character and discipline our thinking, forcing us to push beyond our circumstances and grapple with the world of possibility because there is no turning back. And so, it was that Robin faced each new day with that mixture of fear and hope, uncertainty and promise. They were the new realities that kept her company in the silent recesses of her own heart. Through the constant love and support of those around her, the revelation of her accident and attending injuries were brought to light and yet no one spoke the word paralysis, a crushing blow no one was willing to levy against her burgeoning recovery. That revelation could wait until she was stronger.

Two weeks after his initial visit to Robin's bedside, Gary now found himself once again moving down the hospital corridors toward her room. This time with the aid of a cane and soft cast wrap on his leg. He limped along with an odd gait, but was so grateful to be walking again at all, that he ignored the stares of others as he hobbled along. Nearing her door, he noticed a nurse was giving Robin her medications while discussing her therapy options. He leaned up against the wall for support and waited for the nurse to leave. As he stood there, he rehearsed in his mind all the things he planned to say to her and the things he would not say at first. He would try to learn more about her from their conversation and gathered clues as to how to help in her recovery. Once the coast was clear, he walked in bolstered by a false sense of bravado he didn't really feel. Robin looked up from the book in her lap to see who was coming, and looked puzzled, so he smiled and said hello as he inched toward her bed. She cocked her head to one side with a suspicious look on her face; it was as if she knew him, but couldn't quite remember from where or when. Then it came to her, he was the man in a wheelchair beside her bed that late afternoon when she first opened her eyes. Yes, this was the first face she had seen and then he had disappeared without a word and was gone. At first, she wondered if she had imagined him, but as time moved on his image faded and he was forgotten. Now here he was again, this time without the chair and slightly unsteady, but none the less here. Before she could say a word, he told her his names was Todd Harmon and that he'd heard about her terrible accident during his own hospital stay. Being somewhat banged up himself, he wanted to come by to wish her well and see how she was doing. Her soft, brown eyes looked him over as she wondered why this perfect stranger would know of her accident and care enough to make two visits to check on her.

Gary realized he must keep his true identity a secret for the time being, or risk losing further access to Robin. He of all people would be an unwelcomed guest in her room, so he created a new identity as he moved along. He described for her, in the vaguest terms, a fictitious motorcycle accident that put him in a ditch with the motorcycle on top of him, due to a skid out on a slick road. Something like what had actually happened to his cousin Jerry last year. He then turned a concerned look on Robin and asked how she was coming along. Somewhat hesitant, she told him of her overall medical condition, and shared her hopes and desires for a full recovery, while accepting the reality that it may take some time. He encouraged her to describe the accident as she remembered it, surprised to discover she had never even seen him coming as he sped through the intersection. She was there one moment and then she wasn't. All she knew about the accident had come to her secondhand through her parents and the medical staff. As they visited, Gary made every effort to be engaging, his sincere wishes for her well-being were made clear. He tried to lighten the moment with silly jokes about bad hospital food and the difficulty of moving around to take care of necessaries while hooked up to an IV bag on a stand; a badge of courage for any recovering medical patient. He studied her face for any faint flicker of a smile or raised eyebrow, looking for the remotest sign that he was connecting with her.

Just then Robin's parents entered her room surprised to see a strange visitor there. Robin introduced Todd Harmon as the mystery man at her bedside the afternoon she had awakened. With a nod of recognition, her parents recalled that day and apologized for not taking him into account. They explained how overcome with exhaustion and emotion they were when they saw their daughter's eyes open. As Robin explained to her parents the reason for Todd's visit, Mr. and Mrs. Walker thought it was very kind and thoughtful that this man who obviously had a heart for people and an easy congenial manner would take the time to inquire about their daughter who was now smiling. Gary looked at Robin and said he should go, for he didn't want to tire her out but wondered if he might pop in again sometime, for his office was downtown near the hospital. Yet another lie he would need to flesh out at a later date. Surprised at this, Robin said "Yes." Gary reached for Robin's hand and gave it a quick pat as he looked deep into her eyes and spoke of her courageous spirit that wanted to live and that he knew with certainty God had his eye on her. The warmth of his smile and glimmer of moisture in his eyes touched Robin's heart and at that very moment a tender bond was formed. With goodbyes all around, Gary moved toward the door turning one last time for a quick wave and was gone. Now limping down the hall, he felt as if his heart was pounding out of his chest; as his head reeled from a flood of converging thoughts and feelings.

In the next few weeks, Gary visited Robin often. Watching her flower unfurl as she became stronger, her internal damage slowly mending, tissue and bone knitting back together, some bodily functions now willing to work on their own. During this critical time of restoration, two battered hearts and souls tentatively reached out to one another and ultimately found safe harbor; as a tight bond was formed out of the wreckage of their lives. During Gary's visits they cautiously shared their personal anguish about the damage done to their young bodies, hoping it could be overcome and their lives could be put back together. The fears, hopes, and dreams each had in the days before them were openly discussed and pondered. As the ease and the trust of their friendship grew, there came moments of actual laughter and the discovery of joy in the moments that transcended circumstance; a healing balm lifting their spirits, opening a new vision of possibility that lay in waiting. Gary's visits often coincided with other friends and family members with whom he became acquainted and was soon taken into their inner circle. Robin's parents in particular noticed the positive effect Gary's friendship had on their daughter's recovery and were delighted to see him each time he appeared. They also noticed Robin's room was now filling up with flowers, funny cards and the occasional balloon sporting a smiley face or some snappy retort to make Robin giggle. Looking back to the fateful day of their accident, one would have never dreamt those two strangers, who collided in such a death-defying moment, would emerge from that devastation to become a life raft for one another, a way home from the edge of a dark chasm that had nearly devoured them.

Gary arrived late one afternoon to find Robin's parents in a huddle around their daughter, who now sat in a wheelchair near the window, the pale light casting long shadows across the room. As they murmured to one another, Mrs. Walker kissed her daughter's cheeks and wiped at her tears that now came in deep, uncontrollable sobs, catching Robin's breath as she shuddered in her chair. Mr. Walker knelt in front of Robin, holding her small hands in his own while speaking soft, reassuring words of encouragement. As Mrs. Walker looked up, she saw Gary standing in the doorway taking in the scene, a look of concern washed his face. Gary moved across the room slowly, as Mrs. Walker explained to Robin that Gary had come and that they were going to step out for a moment so they could visit. With one last tender hug from her father, Robin adjusted herself in her chair, while wiping at her face, now red from crying. As the Walkers made for the door, Gary and Robin's dad exchanged a knowing look, as they clasped each other's shoulders at passing. Initially, Robin looked away, out of the window, wishing she could escape and fly away from her life, her chair, and the scrutiny of Gary's eyes as he put down his cane and settled in beside her. At first, they sat in silence for a while, neither saying a word as the sun sank beneath the horizon, leaving them fixed in their private thoughts, now bathed in twilight. Finally, Robin turned her gaze from the window and sought Gary's eyes, while trying to speak through trembling lips that were hesitant to utter the awful truth held secret, for once released it would become a nightmare reality to be dealt with. Once again, her face crumpled as her pleading eyes looked at Gary, searching for relief from the words that choked her, that could find no voice. At that point, Gary reached out for her, as she leaned forward and collapsed on his chest. This was the second time he had ever touched her, other than a pat on the hand a few weeks ago, and now he stroked her head and held her in his arms as best he could, letting her emotions drain, absorbing the blows to her battered body and soul that were, in fact, his own. The bitterness of her anguish swept over him, the cause and effect of a careless moment. Eventually, Robin lifted her head and told Gary she had been with her doctors that afternoon, and undergone extensive testing that determined she would never walk again.

For the next two weeks, Robin rode the roller coaster of emotions that all patients go through when forced to grapple with life-changing realities that can no longer be denied. She exhibited all of the stages of mourning for her past life, now marred and gone forever. Her adamant denial that her wheelchair was indeed going to be a lifelong appendage she could not function without, made her seem irrational at times, followed by accusing fits of rage against God, fate, and life in general, that when over, left her limp, totally spent, and feeling helpless. Then there were the days of muted depression, when she did not speak or eat and tears ran in silent streams down a face, devoid of any signs of expression or emotion, when she was trapped in the bottom of a deep, dark pit, unable to muster the will to climb back out. Gary, along with Robin's family, was highly concerned for her ultimate well-being and struggled to keep a positive spin on her future, as they worked through the very real issues of validating Robin's pain and suffering. The precarious balance between compassion and hope was a tightrope they would collectively march across together. Gary was a witness to and participant in, all of the transitioning episodes Robin went through. At every turn, he had been there, by her side, to empathize, strategize, and cajole her along to a rational, realistic acceptance of her situation, for only then would come the true and sustainable healing of her body, mind, and spirit. On one such morning, Gary arrived at the hospital to surprisingly discover a quantum leap had been made in Robin's psyche. She seemed to be reinvigorated with a new sense of self that was not going to let a wheelchair define her. The anger she had once exhibited, now turned into a fire-in-the-belly kind of determination, to take back her life even if she had to do it on wheels. Acceptance and resignation had finally come, the desire for life, on any terms, had won out over the acquiescence to fear and despair. Gary, reeling from the sly smile now seen on Robin's face, was born again into the hope of a future he had only prayed would be possible for Robin, and, now, he could not separate himself from that future, for out of the darkness and horror of the accident, and all they had shared since then, had evolved an abiding trust at such a deep, personal level of intimacy, that their hearts now beat with one accord. They had fallen in love. Her willingness to now look forward was truly a godsend, a corner turned that now led to a path of hope, renewal, and, yes, even gratitude.

During the weeks of concern and caring for Robin Walker, Gary had also dealt with the death of his own marriage to Sheryl, an inevitable conclusion to their deteriorating relationship that left them with the inability to even have a civil conversation, their divorce ultimately brokered by their two attorneys. The final disillusion of the marriage had come in the wake of Robin's collapse over the news concerning her permanent paralysis. The combined weight of these concerns bore down on Gary, as he also struggled to get back on his feet at work, while maintaining his false identity with Robin. The many complications of his life were bittersweet on many levels but, through it, he had emerged a better man with a new sense of purpose that guided him mostly by intuition, toward an uncharted destiny, aided by the compass of his own heart to help him find his way.

The largest obstacle in Gary's immediate future was to find a means to bridge the gap between his longing to be with Robin the rest of his life, while reconciling the past by telling her and her parents of his real identity. As he paced up and down on the deck in his sunny garden one morning, he held to the rail for added support, his nervous energy set on full throttle by the three cups of coffee he had consumed on an empty stomach. Back and forth, he went pondering his demise. He wondered if what he and Robin had built between them could withstand a betrayal of this proportion. He just didn't know. He did, however, know one thing for sure, if he had confessed who he was at first, he would never have been allowed to see Robin again, and that just wasn't an option he could accept. How could he make Robin and her parents understand the total devastation and fear he felt when he had first seen Robin laying there in a coma, barely clinging to a life he had nearly destroyed? How could he adequately explain the sense of responsibility he felt that would not allow him to just turn and walk away, and then with all they had shared over time, turning into love and appreciation for this remarkable woman that had been placed in his life. Plopping down on a deck chair, Gary gazed out over the yard, watching the birds skitter under the sprinkler then dash off to fluff their feathers. If he could only shake off these feelings of indecision as easily, he would be so relieved. But the moment of truth had finally come, and he had no choice but to move forward.

The family initially decided Robin might do better adjusting to her new situation at her parent's home, where she could receive help and support as she learned to live with the new parameters of her disability. She returned to her childhood room in the rambling Spanish, stucco home in Tampa, where she had grown up and knew every nook and cranny by heart. A health-aid worker came to the home and taught her some new maneuvers with her chair that would accommodate the necessary routines of living, hygiene, and movement from her chair to her bed. As she practiced the regimen each day, she became stronger and more confident. On a clear, warm night, steeped in the fragrance of bougainvillea that grew by the pool, Gary found Robin on the veranda with a tumbler of iced tea in her hand, and a fat cat on her lap. She looked up and smiled, waving hello, as Taffy, a striped tabby, jumped up and made a mad dash for cover in the nearby bushes, having never been fond of strangers. As Gary greeted her with a sweet kiss, she threw her arms around his neck to steal another. While pulling up a chair closer to hers, Gary let out a relaxed sigh, as he sat down and reached for her hand, asking about her day. For the next two hours, they sat talking, laughing, and teasing each other. It came so natural and easy between them, a comfortable fit that had never been forced or contrived. It was on this perfect, warm, summer evening that Gary turned to Robin and said he loved her more than he thought it possible to love another, and that he would have no life without her in the center of it, and would she please consider a proposal of marriage as his total commitment to her and the feelings he hoped she shared. As the big, yellow moon rose over the tree tops, beyond the rippling pool, tears filled Robin's eyes as she looked at Gary with mixed emotions. Oh, how she had come to love him for the selfless way he had made her troubles his own, and never failed to show up and cheer up a bad situation when she needed a lift. But, what about him? Didn't he deserve a whole person as a wife and partner through life, someone who could offer him all the normal things he needed and desired that she could not deliver? She couldn't bear the thought that he just felt so sorry for her that he was willing to throw away his own life on someone so needy. As she tried to express these sentiments, Gary would have none of it. He moved his chair to face her and taking both of her hands in his own, he implored her to never misinterpret his love for pity, and that he had fallen head over heels for a whole, beautiful, sweet, intelligent woman that he needed by his side, no matter what the future may bring. By now, the tears she had tried to restrain ran freely down her cheeks, as she opened her arms to return his embrace and said "Yes."

In the weeks following Gary's proposal, wedding plans were discussed with the usual excitement and anticipation. Robin's parents seemed delighted with the prospects of expanding their small family circle to include a son-in-law, especially as they had come to know and love Todd Harmon for all the care and tenderness he gave their daughter during the most critical juncture of her life. An engagement party was being planned to announce the coming nuptial. The celebration was to be held at a local neighborhood restaurant with a small number of family and friends in attendance to share a special meal and champagne toast to the happy couple. As the long warm days of summer lingered, now June, soon to be July; the balmy weather seemed perfect for a beautiful, garden ceremony at the Walker home in Tampa, scheduled for the first weekend in August. And so it was that plans were laid in joy, with everyone looking forward to a day all would have considered lost only a few weeks ago. Gary was amazed how quickly things were coming together, and he too looked forward with longing to the day he would have Robin all to himself; to freely plot their course, secure in the love and warmth of their unique friendship now in full bloom. But amid the up and coming festivities remained the looming issue of a truth untold. Now with the full assurance of Robin's committed love and her parents' acceptance of their pending marriage, Gary fought with himself over how and when to unveil his secret. A secret that had the power to derail and totally destroy forever, all he now hoped for. God had been gracious by giving him and Robin a second chance at life; would he now also manifest a miracle of forgiveness? Could love and restoration be sustained in the face of falsehood, regardless of the motivations? Could the ends justify the means in this case? Character and honor were two virtues Gary had been taught in his youth, especially as they affected the lives of others. He knew he would never have inner peace or freedom in his soul while he lived a lie.

July tenth had been selected as the date for the announcement dinner at Fernando's Italian Bistro. The intimate, small restaurant had been totally reserved for the Walker family that night, who had been neighborhood friends of the establishment for the last twenty years. Anna and Marco Angelino, the owners of the Bistro, had known Robin since childhood; Marco being the one who taught Robin at the age of eight to eat her spaghetti by twirling it on the end of her fork. Anna was elated to be included in the Walker's plans for dear Robin, as she selected special linens for the occasion, and glowing globes surrounded with sweet, white Gardenias and pale, pink Hibiscus that would come from her own garden. Gary knew he could not endure the evening as the anxious, adoring groom with a heart full of deceit. With the announcement night just a week away, the time to come clean had arrived. As he called Robin and made arrangements to come by and discuss their wedding plans with both she and her parents, he prepared to walk a gauntlet of his own making, praying that divine intervention would prevail where he could not. At half past seven that night, Gary paced up to the Walkers' door and rang the bell. He felt as if his heart was in his throat and he could barely exhale from the nervous tension he felt. This was the most important make or break moment of his young life; his entire future and happiness was now riding on an outcome uncertain.

After Gary rang the bell, Mr. Walker appeared at the door, a broad smile on his face as he welcomed Gary in with a warm, manly bear hug. Joyful greetings were made all around as Gary saw Robin in her chair in the living room, with out-stretched arms beckoning his embrace, her heart light glowing in her eyes. A tray with large glasses of iced tea and fingers of shortbread was placed on the coffee table of the comfortable room and cozy chairs had been pulled up snug for easy conversation. As everyone settled in a seat, Gary took an end of the sofa next to

Robin's chair and reached for her hand. She smiled her warm response as the casual banter of conversation followed. Mrs. Walker was the first to inquire as to what concerns or ideas Todd may have regarding the wedding, indicating they were all interested in receiving his input. Readjusting himself in his chair, Gary looked intently into the eyes of all assembled and with a silent plea for mercy, began. His first comments were of a reassuring nature, explaining his total commitment to Robin whom he regarded as an extraordinary and wonderful young woman and how he was so fortunate to have her in his life. He described that what had started out as a congenial friendship had developed into so much more. He then rushed on to the beginning, describing his feelings at first seeing Robin, comatose and bedridden; and then it came, with a pained look on his face he told them he had initially been so interested in Robin because he was the man driving the white SUV that had plowed through the intersection that fateful Saturday morning and had nearly taken Robin's life. Immediately the air was sucked out of the room as a moan came from Robin who was now bent over in her chair, hiding her face with her hands as she began to weep. Mrs. Walker, with a stricken look on her face immediately ran from her chair to comfort her daughter as Mr. walker got up from his seat putting both hands in his pockets and walked to the front window gazing out in total disbelief and shock, overwhelmed beyond words.

Gary moved on telling of the horror and fear he had felt when he saw the extent of the damage one careless act had caused and he had used the cover name of Todd Harmon in order to see Robin and monitor her progress; the heavy weight of his responsibility in this matter soon became his primary focus, with a deep desire to help right the wrong that had been done if that were even possible. Gary paused to wait for this sad information to be fully digested.

The tension in the room was palpable and oppressive, hanging in the terrible void of silence. Finally, Robin wiped at her eyes, fingers trembling, as her mother moved away and taking Mr. Walker by the arm, they quietly left the room. Two hearts and souls that had been slowly mending, healing through the bond of their common suffering now found new depths of sorrow never intended or anticipated. Love had caught them off guard and a simple convenient deception had now become an arrow to pierce the heart. For the next hour Gary spoke in hushed tones to Robin, explaining in detail his true identity, his life with Sheryl, and the unhappy divorce. He told her about the terrible argument he had with her on the cell phone the morning of the accident when he angrily pushed through the yellow light never seeing her car move into the intersection. He told her about his business and home, while he patiently answered every question she asked. Toward the end of their exhausting session riddled with accusations, countered with pleading for forgiveness and followed by more tears concerning issues of trust now shattered, the two were spent.

Everything had been laid bare on the table, unembellished for a closer look. But the one resounding theme through it all was Gary's total love and unwavering commitment to Robin the woman he loved and would always love, no matter what she decided to do. He now reached for her hand again that she only tentatively allowed him to touch, her sober expression speaking volumes about the condition of her battered heart. It was decided that a few days of separation to think things through was warranted and that she would call him when she was ready to discuss things further. He gently kissed the limp hand he held and without another word rose to leave. Out in the street he wandered to his car where he sat paralyzed and wounded, wondering how he was going to live without her.

The next week was a torturous time for both Gary and Robin, each was caught up in their individual world of doubt, fear, and anxiety. For Robin, the revelation that the man she had befriended, then came to know and love, was indeed the very man who had irresponsibly changed her life forever, was totally horrific. She spent her days weighing the deceit and awful truth against all the love and tenderness she had been shown; all this by the same man she thought she knew and trusted. Robin had long discussions with her parents and a very best friend whom had been sworn to secrecy about the betrayal. In her sleepless nights she tossed and turned, her restless heart plagued with conflicting emotions and indecision. Finally, in her total exhaustion and despair, she turned to prayer and begged God to help her take the right course, one that would affect the rest of her life. Eventually, on Thursday evening, just two days before their announcement party at the Bistro, Robin came to a place of peace in her heart and mind as she picked up the phone to call Gary. She needed to have this conversation with him, to put things into a rational perspective so she could move on with her life.

When Gary picked up the phone, he was thrilled to hear Robin's voice. He had been so afraid she might never choose to speak with him again. However, he did notice that her speech was very somber and businesslike as she asked him to drop by on his lunch hour on Friday and that what she had to say would not take long so he could return to work. Her cool resolution shot a pang of grief through his body as he agreed to the meeting and hung up the phone. Gary paced his house until the wee hours of the morning wondering what Robin was going to say and if there was anything left for him to tell her that could make a difference now. In the blush of dawn Gary sat in his kitchen staring into the deep void of his coffee cup asking himself, How had it all come to this. With elbows planted on the table, he clasped his hands together, and lowered his head and began to implore God for help, along with expressing his need for mercy and forgiveness. He also prayed for the grace to accept Robin's verdict concerning the future of their relationship if there was to be one. He knew he had done the right thing by confessing his deception and now had to be prepared to accept the consequences of his actions no matter the outcome.

Friday at noon, Gary appeared at the door of the Walkers' home. He rang the bell and as he stood waiting, he nervously fidgeted with something in his left pocket while trying to put on a pleasant, calm demeanor. It was Mr. Walker who opened the door, his face expressionless as he invited Gary in and announced his arrival to Robin who sat in her chair in the living room, where they had all sat together just a few days before to hear Gary's news. With pale light from the window bathing Robin's figure and serene countenance, Gary thought he had never seen her look more beautiful and radiant than she did at that moment. All of this tore at his broken heart. As he neared her chair and shyly said hello, she looked up at him, her soft, brown eyes searching his face, as if really seeing him for the first time. Mr. Walker watched Gary get settled then quickly left the room giving his daughter privacy to deal with the matter at hand.

Gary sat on the edge of his seat facing Robin. He leaned forward resting his elbows on his spread knees and webbed his fingers together as he studied his feet for a few moments then looked up to meet her gaze. She began to speak slowly, never losing eye contact with Gary as she described in detail the tumultuous week she had endured and the pain of working through her emotions, sorting them out, measuring them against the facts as she knew them now. The more she spoke, her gentle eyes began to brim with tears that further pierced Gary's soul. Robin explained that she had prayed for wisdom that God would show her what would be best for her in the long run and she felt sure that God had given her a clear answer.

With a pleading heart, Gary then asked her what she and God had decided. As one single tear escaped her eyes and rolled down her soft cheek, she reached out to him with both arms open wide and said, "I love you, I need you, I want you."

Gary instantly fell to his knees before her chair and was wrapped in the warmth of her embrace as they then clung to each other and wept with relief. God had stepped into the breach once more with these two young lives and performed another miracle, one of forgiveness, tenderness, and restoration. Seeking Gods face, they sidestepped the misery of a life lived in sorrow, full of regret and had instead chosen love, that God has told us through his word, is transforming and transcendent. Robin and Gary chose to take that path.

Now freed from their position of eavesdropping, around the corner in the dining room, Robin's parents quietly emerged walking into the living room they moved toward the reunited couple, placing their arms around them, kissing away their tears. After composure was regained by all, an announcement was made by Mrs. Walker that a special lunch had been laid on the dining room table and that they should move that way and be refreshed. Later as the dishes were cleared and a light dessert was served, Gary stood up and said he had planned something for Saturday night at the Bistro, but under the circumstances, he didn't want to wait. From out of his left pocket, he pulled a beautiful diamond ring and placed it on Robin's slender finger accompanying the gesture with a tender kiss. Through the joy of clapping hands, and a few "Ooh's" and "Aah's," more hugging ensued.

Saturday night at the Bistro was in every way a delightful celebration of the triumph of love over circumstance. The happy couple seemed more infatuated than ever before, as all the usual pre-wedding congratulations were expressed. All the women gathered around Robin to inspect the dazzling brilliance of her gorgeous ring while the men engaged in back slapping and inquiries about their honeymoon plans. The restaurant glowed in soft candlelight, beautiful quiet music played in the background and the sweet fragrance of fresh cut flowers rose from the center of each table. The warmth of love and friendship filled the air at this special gathering that almost did not happen.

In the following month of August, the balmy summer weather with its slight breeze off Tampa Bay was perfect for their evening wedding.

The Walkers' garden had been completely transformed with a look of elegant enchantment. Yards of soft lavender bunting tied up with bright green fern, white roses and lavender satin ribbon framed the isles of seating and arched around the central trellis where the pastor stood ready to pronounce God's holy ordinance on their behalf. As the couple completed their vows, each added their own personal pledge of devotion to one another. The food, fun, and toasting went on as the bouquet was thrown and caught and the cake was cut. The flung garter landed in the pool while all laughed and no bachelor offer to go in and claim it.

Later that night as the couple made their getaway, family and friends waved them off, wishing them well. Gary's sedan that had been decorated earlier in the day with a "Just Married" sign and colored streamers now moved through the darkened street and out of sight toward a future the happy couple just claimed for their own. As Robin nestled next to Gary, her head on his shoulder, they talked and laughed quietly about the day neither of them would ever forget. The only people who knew where Robin and Gary were going were Robin's parents, who were touched by the irony of their destination. When Gary had asked Robin where she might like to honeymoon, she responded with a quizzical smile on her face and said she would really like to stay at her favorite bungalow at St. Pete Beach, a place she had always loved and was headed for the day of their accident. And so it was, that Gary's car glided north in the moonlight, up the Gulf Coast road toward the beach. Late in the afternoon of their first day alone together as man and wife, Robin was on the beach adorned with her hot pink visor, sunglasses and a tumbler of iced tea. Soon Gary plopped down beside her and after stealing a kiss, announced that the shrimp kabobs she had been dreaming of would soon be ready.

Later that night as they lay in each other's arms on the deck of their bungalow, under the starry sky listening to the rush of the surf pushed by the incoming tide, they discussed plans for their immediate future. They would live in Gary's house that they would remodel to accommodate Robin's needs and she would be given *carte blanche* to decorate it to suit her good taste and sense of style.

Robin expressed her gratitude for the great company she had worked for, whose senior management had stayed in contact with her all these months, monitoring her progress. They told her they fully appreciated her talent and skills and would love to have her back whenever she felt ready. As the two held each other tight and reflected on all that had happened to them, they were truly amazed that out of the deepest darkest moments of their lives, God had brought two unlikely souls together in an unimaginable way and through their struggles had blessed them both with each other. They had matured through their ordeal of suffering and come to a hard-won wisdom that would serve them well the rest of their lives. God placed before them life and death and they had chosen life.

Not looking forward to the future without his wife and sweetheart Genie, Hack Henshaw struggles to find his way as a single person in his later years, when out of the blue he hears from an old friend he hasn't seen in years. Reunited through the fun of their shared past, Hack is invited to take part in a fabulous adventure that will inadvertently enrich the vitality to his altered life. Read **Never Say Die** to discover that where there is life, there are always new possibilities.

NEVER SAY DIE

*A*mong the relics of "Old South Town," a small enclave in the South Carolina low country, sat "Bull" Hack Henshaw, seated on the patio of his favorite bistro fingering a frosted glass of iced tea and wondering where time had gone. His peevish grin revealed a thoughtful regard for his past that had run headlong into his future and never looked back. Now, newly acquainted with retirement, his reflections were a mixed bag of ambitions, a few disappointments, plenty of drive and sometimes misguided passions that had all lead to a fulfilling, adventurous life. Now from his vantage point, a small table nestled between two potted palms, he reminisced, scrolling through his memories while chuckling to himself. It was almost as if his past belonged to someone else and he was merely an observer.

Hack Henshaw acquired the nickname Bull from his family who had chided him since childhood for his bulky physique and total lack of grace. He had been the proverbial "bull in the china shop," always bumping into things, tripping, and knocking things over. However, as Bull matured, luckily, so did his body and coordination, but by then the name had stuck!

Bull sat sipping at his drink and enjoying the quiet when he noticed someone approaching his table. Oh no, he thought. It was Alisha Morris, a desperate, middle-aged widow who had been stalking him ever since his own dear wife Genie passed away two years ago.

"Hi Bull," she hollered and waved, while she strolled to his table and sat her more than ample derriere in the adjacent seat. "Where have you been?" she inquired. "Tuesday, we were in need of a fourth for pinochle and you were nowhere to be found," she said with a sly grin as she rolled her eyes. "Shame on you," she sighed. "Have you been hiding?"

Bull could only stammer and mumble something about bass fishing out of state with some buddies. Alisha, not to be dissuaded, pressed on with a dinner invitation for the next Thursday night.

Bull said, "Dinner would be great but I'll have to take a rain check for now, and I'll be in touch."

As Alisha rose from the table, she winked at Bull and told him not to wait too long because neither of them were getting any younger. Bull saluted and smiled as she turned to walk away.

Bull worked for years in the aeronautics industry as an engineering consultant after a short stint as a bomber pilot with the US Air Force during the Vietnam War. He had lived all over the world and had developed a taste for the exotic. It was in his mid-thirties when he met Genie Horner, who was working as an attaché for the US Embassy in Cairo, Egypt. He noticed her right off and pursued her in earnest during his deployment in the Middle East. They hiked among the pyramids, sailed the Nile and shopped the colorful markets in search of treasure. The carefree days of their early courtship were magical and he never tired of savoring those moments, especially now that Genie was gone. They had an idyllic marriage as the best of friends and he still missed her terribly. Their forty-seven years together had blessed them with two beautiful, bright daughters, Amy and Nicole who were now middle-aged women with families of their own. Since their mother's passing, however, they hovered around Bull like he was some sort of adolescent who had lost his way and needed their direction. He tolerated their mothering good naturedly because he loved them both so much and felt a special connection to his sweetheart Genie every time he was with them.

Now set with the task of reinventing himself as a 70-year-old, single person, Bull turned his attention to filling his days with various diversions to keep from feeling so alone. He had worked on his golf game, finished restoring his old antique MG sports car he picked up overseas and was trying to learn Spanish.

"El sol todavía está brillando," which means "The sun is still shining." And that is how Bull felt about life. There could still be good days with wonderful things to enjoy. He had to find a new way to keep going, to keep doing what he had always done…and maybe more.

One Sunday afternoon, while Bull was halfway dozing in his recliner and watching a football game on TV, his beloved Gamecocks holding a fragile lead over the Georgia Bulldogs, his phone rang. When he said hello, he was so surprised to hear the voice of his old buddy Reggie Newsom who was a long-time divorcee, whom he hadn't seen in years. Again, Bull was reminded of how time slips through the hourglass and how we are left looking back. After the usual pleasantries and catching up with one another's lives, Reggie got right to the point of his call. In the mischievous voice Reggie was noted for, he told Bull that he was now working on his bucket list and wondered if Bull still had one more adventure in him because he couldn't do this without Bull Hack Henshaw in the mix.

"What on earth are you talking about?" said Bull.

"Do you remember", said Reggie, "that time we were down in Bogotá, Columbia, training their Air Guard how to operate those F-15 Eagle Tactical Fighters our government sold them and how we would take long weekends and go sailing off the coast?"

"Sure, I remember," said Bull. "We had quite a time the twelve months we were down there."

"Well," said Reggie, "I have always wanted to go back to Columbia. Over the years, the country has developed one of the largest ship building industries in the world outside of Asia."

"So what does that have to do with your bucket list?" asked Bull.

"Well I was coming to that," said Reggie.

"It just so happens that one of the major titans in the ship building industry in Columbia is a man by the name of Juan Fernando. It seems he has a passion for old sailing ships and has built himself a replica of the Cutty Sark, a British clipper ship. The original was built on the River Clyde in 1869 and was used to ship tea all over the world. It was the fastest sailing vessel of its kind before steam propulsion became popular. Another buddy of mine, Hank Pierce, who also loves to sail, heard through the grapevine that Fernando is putting together an international crew to take his ship, the Cutty II, out for her maiden voyage and sail her from Buenaventura on the west coast of Columbia, around the horn, the tip of South America, and up to Rio de Janeiro in Brazil. I think it will be a blast. Hank and I have already decided to go, and of course I thought of you. We absolutely have to do this Bull. It's going to be a fabulous trip!"

Three months later, Reggie, Bull, and Hank stepped off the plane in Bogotá, Columbia, and into the acute heat and humidity of the South American summer in late January. They rented a car and began traveling southwest toward the coast and Buenaventura, where they would hook up with Fernando and the rest of the crew at the Danesta Hotel next to the harbor.

The hotel was an enchanting place, set against the lush, tropical landscape, with its dramatic Spanish architecture and ornate iron grill work. After checking in, they were directed to a lavish reception area where the rest of the crew was gathered. Juan Fernando was a middle-aged man of medium stature with a taught, muscular physique. His short, silver hair was slicked back and in deep contrast to his bronze skin and keen, dark eyes. His heavy accent worked its way past the large Cuban cigar that hung from his lips unlit. As the three approached the group, Fernando was laughing and wildly gesturing with his arms as he entertained everyone with a fish story about a blue marlin he had hauled in from the warm waters of the Pacific.

Soon the head maître d' signaled to Fernando that the private dining room was ready to serve dinner, a wonderful feast of the Columbian cuisine. The main course consisted of a traditional favorite Bandeja Paisa, an interesting mix of white and red beans, shredded meat, pork rind, black pudding, fried egg, avocado, and plantains.

After dinner, the host Fernando stood to his feet and offered a toast to the new crew of the Cutty II and a blessing for safety and smooth sailing on their epic voyage. There was the clanking of glasses and hoots and shouts from the crew as they lifted their goblets and drank their champagne. Fernando then had each man introduce himself and tell about his sailing experience and why he was interested in making this voyage. The men were an amazing mix of cultures and backgrounds, but the single common denominator was their love for the sea and sailing.

There were two men from Nova Scotia who had worked the North Atlantic as fisherman. Three men were from England and had skulled down the Thames while in college and then did a short stint in the Royal Navy. Four men were from Trinidad and had spent their entire lives on the sea. Two others were from Venezuela who ran a small commercial shipping company that exported home commodities down the river Rio Orinor to remote towns in Brazil's vast Pontanal, the rainforest wet lands. Fernando's brother Samuel was also to be a part of the crew. He was a jovial character who owned a dive shop in Cali where he gave scuba diving lessons and offered dive excursions off the coast. He had held a NAUI certification for over twenty years and was an extremely skilled deep-water diver. Then of course there were the three Americans, two of which were hobbyist sailors, Bull and Reggie. Hank, however, had in past years been involved with the Americus Cup competitions and had actually sailed with a crew one season that came in second place. It was through Hank's connections in the sailing world that he heard about Cutty II.

Fernando then explained that the Cutty was in dry dock just south of them in the port city of Machala and that the group would travel there tomorrow for the official christening and launch. He handed each man a picture of the Cutty II with a schematic of her lower decks. Each man had been given an assigned position and task, with their sleeping billets and stow holds circled in red.

The next morning was filled with excitement and anticipation as the crew packed their gear and climbed aboard the two waiting vans that would carry them to Machala and the Cutty II. When the crew finally reached their destination in the early afternoon; each man was thrilled to see the magnificent sailing vessel that was to be his home for the next several weeks. The Cutty II had a long, sleek hull just like the original, 212 feet in length and a sharp bow that could cut through waves. There were three large masts projecting from the hull, the center mast being the tallest at 150 feet high. The Cutty was fitted with eleven miles of rigging that, when used under full sail, could propel the ship at seventeen-and-a-half knots or twenty miles per hour across the open sea. The vessel employed 32,000 feet of canvas sail over her iron frame and wooden hull which made her the fastest sailing frigate of her day, all now to be relived.

As Fernando smashed a magnum of champagne over the Cutty's bow, the ship was released from its moorings and slipped into the harbor. The building of the Cutty II had generated tremendous local interest and the pier was flooded with excited bystanders and well-wishers that day. Cheers rang out and firecrackers exploded as the beautiful new ship settled in the water, while hands on deck worked anchor ropes to position her close to the boardwalk. Soon a gangplank was put in place and all those gathered were invited aboard for a look around. What a fabulous celebration of one man's vision and love for sailing.

The next two days were consumed with provisioning the ship. From bow to stern, stow holds to galley, the ship was fully equipped. Finally, the morning of departure arrived and the dawn was a spectacle of color. Gorgeous clouds of gold, purple and pink streaked the sky and hugged the horizon, while the sun like a giant fire ball climbed in the distant mist. The pier was once again filled with spectators, there to view the Cutty's official send off. An anthem was played and flags were waved as the ship slowly sailed from the still waters of the harbor, to slice the waves of the open sea.

The first day under full sail was highly exhilarating for both captain and crew. Each man was busy learning his job and station that in turn would be handled in rotation. Some were assigned the riggings up top, others the ballasts below. Some studied charts and the compass while others learned to handle the wheel. It was also a delightful surprise when the crew discovered that Fernando's brother Samuel was a wonderful cook and that he and two hirelings would be taking charge of the galley and meals. That first evening at sail, after a delicious and satisfying supper, the crew filed up on deck to enjoy the cool breeze under a spectacular canopy of stars. The wondrous Orion, Scorpius, and Lepus were among the plethora of constellations that hung in full view. Oh, the joy of the smell of the salt and the open sea.

South ever southward, the Cutty was pushed by prevailing winds, skirting the coast of Peru. Now two weeks out on their journey, Bull was taking his turn at the wheel, when he saw something out of the corner of his eye skitter across the main deck then vanish. Curious, Bull called to Hank, who was his relief that day and asked him to take the wheel. Slowly moving toward the main mast, then on to the leeward side of the ship, Bull edged up against a large keg used to hold extra anchor rope. There to his utter disbelief and surprise was a small boy, crouched between the keg and side wall of the ship. As Bull bent down to get a closer look, the boy shot past him like a rocket, then disappeared below deck.

Bull set out to locate Fernando and found him adjusting the riggings on the aft sail, and motioned for him to come down for a moment. Fernando, clenching his unlit Cuban between his teeth, climbed down the ropes and on to the deck. As the two men leaned against a railing, Bull told Fernando about the boy he had seen. To Bulls dismay, Fernando started to shake his head and laugh. He then told Bull, that two days earlier, while Samuel was working in the galley with several pieces of fruit, the entire pile disappeared when he went to the kitchen for a knife.

"It would seem we have a mouse aboard," Fernando said with a grin.

"What sort of bait do you think we could use to catch a mouse like this?" Bull asked with a smirk on his face, remembering his own childhood pranks.

"Well there is one sure fire way," said Fernando. "A bait that has never failed: obleas, a wonderful sweet brown wafer, sandwiched with cheese and rich marmalade. I could have eaten my weight in those things when I was a child. I will have Samuel make a platter of the wafers to leave on the galley table one night, then, we will wait for our mouse to come out of his hole," laughed Fernando.

"Sounds like a plan," said Bull. In hushed tones, Bull asked, "Should I pass the word to the rest of the crew that we have a young stowaway on board, so they can keep an eye out for him?" "Yes," said Fernando, "and if they see him let me know at once."

"Aye, aye, Captain," said Bull as he turned and walked back to the wheel.

It was just a day later, after the evening meal that the crew lingered at table enjoying the camaraderie the group had already formed. Stories were repeated and lies were told in the usual good-natured, seafaring way. The men laughed and cajoled one other in the manner of brothers-at-arms.

Finally, when the dishes were cleared and the galley was emptied and clean, Samuel appeared from the kitchen with a platter of wafers that he placed in the middle of the center table. He then quietly lowered the lights and went back to the kitchen where he hid behind the door. Fernando and Bull, dressed in dark clothing, hid among the recesses of the galley's deep paneled walls and waited. Approximately an hour after the ship was settled and calm, there came a slight rustling from a storage bin at the far end of the galley. Soon a door creaked open and a slight figure tiptoed to the platter of wafers, snatched them up, and quickly retreated back to the storage bin.

Fernando motioned to Bull, who in turn alerted Samuel and the three men converged on the bin at the end of the galley. One quick jerk of the cabinet door shockingly revealed not one boy but two, crouched in the snug space littered with fruit rinds and wafer crumbs. Wild-eyed with fear and panicked at being discovered, the boys instantly threw down their wafers and made a mad scramble past the three dark, hulking figures and dashed to exit the galley door. Further panic set in when the boys realized the door had been rigged to lock. As Samuel moved to flip on the lights, the two small boys stood huddled together, trembling, understanding that they were now surely caught. The men slowly moved in for a closer look at these ragged, thin lads and the harsh realities of poverty and hardship on the streets of Bogota and other Columbian cities became ever more real and haunting.

The boy's large, gaunt eyes nervously darted back and forth as they sized up their captors with a street savvy well beyond their years. Their clothing was filthy, ragged, and worn. Neither boy had shoes to protect his calloused, crusty feet. The smaller child had a bad scrape on one of his legs that now looked infected. The little one kept looking at the older boy, ready to follow his cue, but now no cues were forthcoming. It appeared that the boys may be brothers from the way the older boy, who looked to be ten, protected and sheltered the younger who might have been five. Keeping their distance from the men, the older boy whispered something softly in Spanish to the smaller boy as he began to whimper and complain of his red, inflamed leg.

Finally gathering their wits about them, the men began to converse with the children. Samuel had gone to the kitchen and returned with two cups of cold milk which he encouraged the boys to come and drink. Fernando crouched down low, extending his arms in a sympathetic gesture and explained to the boys in Spanish, that there was no need to be afraid and that no one was going to harm them. He then gently guided them to chairs near a table. The boys eagerly gulped down the refreshing milk and licked at their white mustaches. After feeding the boys a bowl of stew, Samuel returned to the kitchen and closed the door. Fernando and Bull sat with the boys and began to slowly unravel the mysterious back story of these two bedraggled urchins.

It was gradually discovered that the boys were indeed the brothers Sanchez, Nicholas the older and Matisse the younger, whose father had abandoned the family shortly after Matisse was born and whose mother had disappeared one night a year ago, after an abusive fight with her live-in boyfriend. The children had been completely on their own, living on the streets for the past twelve months. It had been a major struggle for these young boys to find safe places to sleep each night and food to eat, all the while hiding from street gangs ready to brutalize or exploit them. The boys were very tired and frightened, looking for an escape when they saw a ship in the harbor.

It was further revealed that the boys boarded the Cutty at Machala, hidden and intermingled among the dense crowd that flooded the ship the afternoon of its christening. Evidently no one saw them, or paid any attention if they did. It was as if the boys were invisible. Lying low until the ship set sail, the boys then moved about the Cutty primarily at night, under the cover of darkness, finding new nooks and crannies to hide in. They scavenged food from the galley when they were hungry and slept most of the day from pure anxiety and utter exhaustion. As time moved on, Nicholas and Matisse were astounded that they had not been discovered, that is until they were!

Scrubbing the boys and doctoring Matisse's infected leg were the first priorities after getting the boys fed. Clean t-shirts were bundled in various ways to cover their skinny little frames and protect them from the sun. Nicholas and Matisse were assigned two bunks that were not in use, where they slept soundly for the first time in months, their fragile lives being rescued by benevolent strangers at a unique time under extraordinary circumstances. The crew was amazed, when introduced to the boys, that they had gone undetected for so many days without ever being spotted by anyone until that fate-filled afternoon when Bull saw something scurry across the deck. By and large, the crew members took a sympathetic view toward the boys. Over the next few weeks as Nicholas and Matisse began to relax and let their individual personalities show, the crew in turn became accustomed to having them on board and began to engage them in conversation and play as time permitted.

Nicholas, the older boy, was the more intense and somber of the two, no doubt because of the responsibility and love he felt for his younger brother. The harsh realities of life at such a tender age had sobered Nicholas and made him serious and guarded. Matisse however, began to blossom like a rose being watered and quickly responded to the provision and kindness that was shown him. Within days he began to smile and laugh. How precious it was to see his young, sweet heart opening to life now that he no longer felt threatened. It was a strange phenomenon but over time, the boys became pets of the crew. One of the English sailors actually suggested that the boys become the official mascots of the Cutty II, the amazing secret cargo of her first voyage.

The deep-water harbor at Valparaiso near Santiago, Chile, was the Cutty's first official port of call; a rustic fishing village tucked among the rocky ledges that littered the Chilean coastline. The village of Valparaiso was beautiful and picturesque with its sunbaked, stucco buildings and red tile roofs, crouched on the edge of the sea, holding the surrounding jungle at bay. There were lush, tropical flowering plants cascading over rocky promontories and a variety of colorful birds fluttering and roosting in nearby trees. Narrow passages etched in the rocks created a network of streets among the shops and homes of the village. The harbor was crowded with a variety of fishing and pleasure craft, so Cutty anchored on the left side of the harbor and the crew launched toward shore in two large rowboats.

Once on land, the locals enthusiastically greeted the crew, for they were totally enchanted at the sight of the Cutty with her tall, majestic, masted sails. Though provisions were needed, along with clothing for Nicholas and Matisse, shopping would only begin after a delightful lunch on the sun-drenched patio at La Mesa (The Table), a wonderful restaurant overlooking the scenic harbor. Delicious food was soon piled high on two trestle tables positioned under a brightly colored awning. The entire crew dove into the steaming food with great relish. Nicholas and Matisse, once gaunt and starved, had fleshed out in recent weeks under the care and feeding of Samuel, and now engaged their appetites along with the rest of the crew. Of course, there was the usual cheerful banter at meal times and this lunch was no exception. Everyone laughed when Bull, who was having fun teasing Matisse, quickly placed a large fried tortilla on Matisse's head and told him to save it as a snack for later. Everyone thought an edible hat was a great idea for a seafaring boy who was always hungry.

Over the two days that followed, the crew enjoyed exploring the village, visiting the shops, joking with the locals and eating delicious exotic food. The proprietors of La Mesa were a warm and engaging middle-aged couple by the names of Sophia and Marco Russo. They had both been very curious about the two young boys traveling with the crew and assumed they belonged to one of the sailors. One afternoon as Fernando was engaging the couple in conversation over a hot cup of espresso, he confessed to them the shocking story of the stowaways and the sad, street life the boys had fled from in Machala. Sophia and Marco were very moved with compassion for the boys and inquired as to what would ultimately happen to the brothers. Fernando, a father himself, said he was very concerned for the boys but had thus far not figured out the end game.

As it happened, Sophia and Marco had tried to have children for several years without success. They had both come from large, robust families and naturally thought that in good time their own home would be filled with the chatter of little ones. Year after year of being childless had left them both with a deepening wound in their hearts. As Fernando described the pitiful condition of the boys when they were found hiding on the ship, Sophia's eyes sparkled with emotion as she looked at Marco who was also moved. As the late afternoon headed toward the dinner hour, Sophia and Marco had to excuse themselves to greet patrons and check on the kitchen. At parting, they told Fernando they would like to speak to him again in the morning before the Cutty's departure.

The next day as the crew gathered up their last-minute supplies, Fernando made his last trip to La Mesa to say goodbye and thank the Russo's for their extraordinary hospitality. As he entered the restaurant, he was warmly greeted by the couple who asked him to sit a moment and they directed him to a quiet table in the corner of the enclosed dining room.

When they were settled in their seats, Marco was the first one to speak. He told Fernando that he and Sophia had been up talking well into the night and had come up with an idea they wanted to share with him. Sophia explained that both she and Marco had always loved children, and had been so disappointed when they were unable to have a family. She went on to describe their spacious home located just up the hill, with a large yard and great garden where they raised their own fruits and vegetables. Marco then said that he and Sophia would love to take the Sanchez brothers and raise them as their own. He told Fernando of their large extended family that could also provide love and protection for the boys into the future.

Marco smiled and said, "We all need family."

Fernando was stunned by the kindness and generosity of this special couple who sat across the table from him, holding hands, and looking imploringly into his eyes. He could tell Sophia would be a tenderhearted mother that would nurture the boys, perhaps in a way they had never known, and help them flourish as young men. Marco was smart, capable, and full of fun. His kind, solid character would be a great example for the boys to follow.

Fernando pushed back from the table and shook his head in wonder. What a wonderful blessing this couple could be for these two lost boys.

He then thoughtfully locked his hands together and looked intently at Sophia and Marco, and asked if they were absolutely sure they wanted to make this enormous commitment? The couple smiled, then nodded yes to one another and then to Fernando.

The next thing to do was to speak to the boys. Fernando went out on the main street and found the brothers in the company of Bull and Reggie, who were about to return to the ship. Fernando called the boys aside and sat them on a street-side bench. Slowly and gently he began to tell them about the rigors at sea during turbulent weather, like they were sure to encounter as they sailed around the horn where they were headed next. He then explained that the weather could often make the water dangerous and unpredictable and that the boys were just too young to be out on the sea under those conditions for what might be days at a time. At this news, the boys looked anxious and uncertain. Fernando went on to reassure them that there was a way they could be secure and out of harm's way.

"And how is that," asked Nicholas, with a slight edge to his voice, while Matisse looked fearfully at his brother's face and then at Fernando's.

"Well," said Fernando, "Marco and Sophia at La Mesa said they would love to have you stay with them." Both boys looked wide eyed at Fernando with sober expressions.

"Can't we come with you?" asked Nicholas in a pleading voice.

"I am afraid not," said Fernando. "But I know the Russo's are kind people and will take good care of you. Why don't we go see them and hear what they have to say?"

Fernando and the boys found the Russo's on the patio at the restaurant. They both joyfully greeted the boys and led them to a table in the shade where cookies and lemonade had been set out. Fernando told the boys that he had a few last-minute errands to take care of and would return in an hour to check on them. He then walked away, leaving the Russo's time alone to bond with the boys.

During Cutty's stay in Valparaiso, the Russo's had opportunities to see the boys and talk with them, creating a sense of fun and friendship. From day one, Marco and Sophia had been welcoming and enthusiastic hosts for the Cutty's crew, especially the two short guys, as Marco fondly named to them. They now explained to the boys more about their home, the restaurant and their lives in general, allowing the boys to ask as many questions as they wanted.

When all of the details had been thoroughly discussed, the Russo's told the brothers they were very special boys and an answer to their prayers. As they hugged Nicholas and Matisse, they reassured them they would be pleased and honored to have them in their home. Now by the time Fernando returned an hour later, it appeared the boys had been won over. Matisse was sitting on Sophia's lap playing a finger game and Nicholas was looking at some picture books and laughing with Marco.

It had been an unpredictable quirk of fate that brought the Sanchez brothers across the path of the ship and crew of the Cutty II, a fate that had unleashed an astonishing, transforming power into the middle of their young lives. The kindness and care received from the crew had eventually led to a greater chance for security, peace and freedom from the poverty and fear that had marked their past. How amazing it was, that through a surprising alliance of four complete strangers, each could now feel complete, whole and loved.

With the entire crew assembled on the pier and ready to launch for the Cutty II, each man had a chance to bid a personal farewell to the boys they had become so fond of. Their hair was tousled and their shoulders squeezed in this last-minute teasing that was now so familiar. The men shook hands with the Russo's and then waved goodbye from the boats as they now made way to the ship. Fernando had been the last of the crew to leave the pier, taking his time in giving thanks to Sophia and Marco for their extraordinary gift of compassion and care. They all laughed and hugged each other, promising to stay in touch, as Fernando finally climbed into the remaining boat. Admonishing the boys one last time to always be good, he raised his hand in a final salute telling Nicholas and Matisse he would always be a part of their lives ... and with that he rowed away.

As the Cutty bore ahead under full sail toward Cape Horn, the most southerly point on the globe, every man of her crew had honed his sailing skills on this large masted vessel and now looked forward with enthusiasm to the next phase of this challenging sea adventure: the fabled horn, the very tip of South America and the Straights of Magellan, that now lay just ahead. Recent hours had been spent hunched over maps and charts, calculating this potentially treacherous part of the voyage. Crew members had heard many stories of other sailors and the folklore seemed consistent with the facts; the horn was replete with wild winds, large waves, and strong currents. This would surely be a great test for this fast frigate, the Cutty II and her able crew. If all went as planned, the Cutty would emerge from around the horn and travel north along the coast of Argentina, then through the straights to Port Stanley in the Falkland Islands, now controlled by the British.

However, it was just off the coast of Punta Arerios, 150 miles north of the horn, when things got interesting. High winds kicked up and began to beat the sea into a virtual froth. Huge rolling waves would crest then crash on to the deck of the Cutty drenching the crew, leaving some clinging to life lines strung along the side walls of the ship to keep men from being washed overboard. Meanwhile others were aloft wrestling with the collapsing sails being tied to their side arms. Fernando and his copilot strained at the wheel to point Cutty's bow into the thunderous waves she was designed to handle. Deepening swells swallowed the ship, then spit her out on the rise of the next cresting wave, a rolling, churning mountain of water.

Over the next forty-eight hours, the fierce weather began to pull Cutty into a chain of strong currents swirling off the tip of the horn, as the crew tried desperately to hold the ship on course and off the rocky shoals; a real test of every man's knowledge of the sea. Hour after hour, crew members manned their positions, fighting the elements and bracing for the worst. The convulsing sea finally tired of its relentless churning near Tierra Del Fuego, when the Cutty made her turn north along the Argentine coast, then northeast to Port Stanley.

Arriving at safe harbor in the Falklands, the crew took a well-deserved rest from their labors and harrowing ride on the rugged sea. The next three days were spent enjoying this unique British colony with its interesting history and traditions. Fernando allowed the inhabitants to visit the Cutty, whose namesake was ever British. Many were fascinated with this elegant ship from antiquity, this floating bit of their own history and wanted their pictures taken with the ship and its crew; for this was a chance meeting, a special moment in time.

Soon the Cutty was under sail again, headed toward Buenos Aires, Argentina, then across the bay to Montevideo, the charming capital city of Uruguay. After two days of re-provisioning the ship, Cutty pressed on further north, to participate in a huge annual sailing event, the Sao Paulo Regatta in Brazil. This spectacular event always attracted a wide variety of sailing craft from all over the region. When the Cutty ll sailed into the harbor, there was a six cannon salute and she instantly became the entire centerpiece of this majestic flotilla. She was the largest and most impressive sailing vessel there and certainly in a class of her own. This exciting four-day festival literally flowed with fabulous food, fantastic fireworks and of course the ever-present rhythmic beat of calypso that pulsed through the air, inspiring dancing, writhing, celebrants along the pier. This regatta was the largest and most famous sailing event in the southern hemisphere each year and a wonderful finish for the Cutty II on her maiden voyage. Under one more day of sail, Cutty would be put in dry dock in Rio, in preparation for another voyage to take place in the spring, a transatlantic sail to England, the home base of the original Cutty Sark.

A Postscript:

Once in Rio de Janeiro, the crew checked into the Hilton on Copacabana Beach and met early the next morning for breakfast to go over the amazing journey they had just completed together. The crew members were now brothers, who would never forget this special time they had shared and their experience with little Nicholas and Matisse, their amazing stowaways. Fernando asked the men if they would be interested in helping with a foundation for the boys, to help fund their college when the time would come and they all enthusiastically agreed. Soon, each man would board a plane and fly home, back to his life as usual, but not without the stunning memories of the past several weeks and the great adventure he had. Bull Hack Henshaw held up surprisingly well on the trip and had such a terrific time that he and Reggie where now returning to their bucket list for further inspiration.

Tess Harper, with her passion for anthropology and professional expertise, inadvertently leads her vacationing family on a quest for adventure and the prospect of solving a mystery associated with an ancient Indian legend. Follow Tess and meet the surprising stranger who helps her decode the secrets hidden in the windswept echoes of time chronicled in **Legends and Legacy**.

LEGENDS AND LEGACY

*H*e leaned in to kiss her, a final gesture of tenderness, holding her brown weathered face in his two hands. Her face was etched with deep furrows, a trail for her tears to follow that had been formed by the recent years of struggle that marked her passage. The astonishment at her circumstances had over time dissolved into anger, then into fear, and ultimately taken their toll on her tired and worn body and soul.

Now hunched down near the open fire, her dim eyes beheld ghostly images of loved ones, ancestors who had gone on before; rising in the curls of smoke and sparks that circled in a high column above her head then disappeared into the dusk. First, there had been the assault on her people and then the decimation of their traditions and very culture. They were driven from their home lands and force marched out into the desolate prairie in the late fall of the year, with few of their own possessions and scant food provisions.

He was now dead, her dear mate Nahan. They had left him strapped to his litter in the dry ravine of an ancient riverbed just two days past where at sunrise, they had torched his pyre and then moved on. The memory of his last kiss would linger in her mind, brushing her cheeks in the soft whisper of the rushing wind never seen only felt. The old Indian woman Awkeen now sat alone; separate from the other migrants making their beds among the sage brush and wild cedar. As she peered into the setting sun, she clutched dried prairie grass in her bent, gnarled hand and began to rock and sing in low haunting murmurs as she fanned the flames of her fire and called on the great spirit of creation to swoop down on majestic eagle wings and carry her away to the place of rest, beyond the moon and stars, to the land of no sorrows.

Tess Harper lowered the book she had been reading based on the eastern and central Indian tribes of the US that had been driven on to reservations during the great western expansion of the 1800s. As she placed the book on her lap, she gazed out the windows that revealed a sweeping panoramic view of the desert that stretched for miles and the red sand stone ledges of the Mesa beyond. Tess had lived her full life of eighty-two years in this region of the Four Corners area in the West, where you can stand in one spot and look into Utah, Colorado, New Mexico, and Arizona all at once. As an anthropologist, she had always been interested in indigenous peoples, their cultures and traditions and so had become enamored with this unique area so rich in Indian history. As Tess removed her glasses and stretched a bit, she realized by a glance at her watch, she had been reading for almost two hours. She had been so absorbed by the narrative about the Indian woman Awkeen that she failed to notice the deepening purple shadows that now painted the steep orange ledges on the horizon. Dusk in the desert was a special time, Tess's favorite part of the day. She got up from her chair in the sunroom and headed to the kitchen where she poured a glass of iced tea and proceeded toward the open deck of her Pueblo-style home to enjoy the light show now in progress.

The tips of the blue sage were drenched in gold while the east side of each bush was awash in a deep shade of hunter green. The ground at their roots was a striation of browns, reds and burnt umber. The mountains to the west of the valley now cast deep shadows over the edges of the desert, their fingers crawling over the landscape, devouring rocky crags and cedars in blue and purple hues. The sky was a contrast of a deepening void with a pale moon rising and a streak of crimson fire that now lit the horizon. As she made her way to a rocking chair near her running fountain surrounded with bright pink bougainvillea, she reflected on God's greatness and his fabulous creation. Tess felt such a sense of gratitude for the life she led here in the splendor of her surroundings. Her thoughts were momentarily interrupted by the hoot of an owl as it settled on the arm of a tall cactus over the dune. Yes, this was God's country and she was glad to be a part of it.

It was late summer, the twenty-third of August to be exact, and though Tess had of recent begun to feel her age, she was still looking forward to one more outing at Lake Powell before winter set in. Her one and only child Matte Harper, was a chemical engineer for a large petroleum company with its base of operations in Phoenix. He had grown up on that lake and loved taking his own family there whenever he could schedule time away from his demanding career. Matte's wife Angie and their two sons, Chad who was twelve and Jordan now fifteen, loved to water ski, swim and fish. They were often affectionately called polliwogs by Grandma Tess for their love of the water. Matte never made plans for a lake trip that didn't include his mother who loved to skim along the surface of the clear blue water and feel the breeze on her face, and besides her good company and interesting chatter, she also brought along many of his favorite camp foods he remembered from childhood. That of course still included s'mores, to be melted over the open campfire. It's funny how some small delights tag along behind us through childhood into our adult lives and never lose their appeal, and in fact become a part of our traditions. So it was that plans were made, that in three days' time, the family would be assembled once more for their last lake trip of the season.

Tess was up early the morning of their departure, moving around her spacious, sunny kitchen where she organized her grub box for the trip, while sipping on a mug of steaming coffee and wondering where she had laid the can opener. Her part of the campout supplies were nearly ready as indicated by the check list she now reviewed and marked with her pencil. Just as she reached for a bag of utensils to put in alongside the cooking pots, her phone rang. Her grandson Chad was on the line to alert her of their eminent arrival and to ask if he could borrow her old Pentax camera for the trip. He wanted to produce a chronicle of their travels and illustrate it with photographs, but his camera was broken. Tess reassured him her camera was available and that she might even have a couple of rolls of film to help with his project.

Signing off, she went to her hall closet and pulled out an old, worn camera bag and located the film. Reaching into its side pocket to find her attachments, her finger fumbled on to a small weathered envelope containing a few old black and white photos. As she gazed at the pictures, a wide grin stretched over her mouth and a giggle escaped her lips. She couldn't really remember the last time she had taken any photos or why she had these pictures pulled aside and placed in her bag, but what fun they were to look at now.

There she was in 1947, leaning up against an old Plymouth coupe in a pair of Bermuda shorts, hiking boots, pith helmet, that looked like a safari hat. She stood with one arm casually thrown around her husband Max, who sat in a camp chair beside her, his own hat cocked in a rakish style like Indiana Jones. He smiled with his pipe dipping the corner of his mouth. They had just come from an archeological dig out in Vernal, Utah, sponsored by the University of Utah, where Max had been the student coordinator for the project. Max and Tess were seniors at the university, when they met, fell in love and later married.

Max, having an affinity for rocks since childhood, had as a normal course been led to the study of archeology, where he would spend the rest of his working years, searching out the creative mysteries of the millennia, trapped in the soil, rocks and sediment of this earthly constellation we call home.

In the next photo, she saw artifacts spread out on a large canvas with Max squatting in the middle, holding what looked to be the substantial remains of a piece of decorative pottery, no doubt made by the Anasazi Indians dating back to between 5500 BC and 700 BC. It was defined by its natural markings and black and white banding. Tess remembered how thrilled she and Max had been at its discovery, it being a remnant of the oldest known, ancient Indian civilizations that had lived in this region of the country. Adding to their pleasure was the size and scale of the piece that from its base was two-thirds complete and in a reasonably good state of preservation. What a treasure. The remains of the find included broken pieces of water jugs, bits of clay pipe and six light spears, two with their flint arrowheads intact. The third remaining photo showed a large pitched tent filled with cots and camping gear, its entire front screened flap unzipped and rolled up to give free access. Alongside the tent was a makeshift trestle table where several tanned and smiling college students posed for their picture to be taken. Some stood nearby holding picks, shovels and brooms, props that defined their tasks each day. *Those were such great times when she and Max had been young and energetic, always looking around the corner for the next new adventure*, Tess reminisced.

There he was, her own dear Max, seated among his minions ever so charming and dapper; the man she had truly loved and adored. At the age of sixty-eight, he had a sudden heart attack in a far-off remote area of Death Valley, where he was surveying and taking soil samples for a paper he was writing. It had come on quickly and passed in a moment before his companions knew he was in any distress. Tess had been without Max for several years now but still warmed to the memory of his boyish exuberance for life and the work he loved. As Tess fingered through the photos one last time when she heard the kitchen door open and close and Matte's familiar voice echoing through the house. As she placed the pictures back in their envelope, she tucked them into her front shirt pocket, then reached for her camera bag and swung it over her shoulder. Making her way up the back hall she grabbed an extra jacket from its peg, remembering that nights on the lake could be cool even in August.

The happy campers left Tess's home in Red Mesa by 6:00 a.m., traveling west on Highway 160 past Monument Valley, then picking up Highway 98 skirting the Hopi Indian Reservation and heading northwest to Page. Upon arriving at Page, everyone was ravenous and excited to visit their favorite Mexican restaurant, Casa Lo-Bo. After a casual refreshing lunch, they wandered outside. From their perch on a high ridge where the restaurant stood, one could see for miles. The travelers stretched and reached for sunglasses while taking in the view. Jordan mentioned that if the Grand Canyon were to ever flood it would look just like Lake Powell, with its steep colorful ledges and sky-blue water. All agreed with nodding heads, then Grandma Tess, ever a treasure trove of trivia, informed the group that it was in 1956 that Congress authorized the building of Glen Canyon Dam to back up the waters of the Colorado, Escalante, San Juan and the Dirty Devil Rivers to create their beloved Lake Powell, and that it took seventeen years to fill it to its present pool of 3,700 feet above sea level.

Chad poked his brother Jordan and said, "No wonder it took us so long to refill our swimming pool last spring when we had to drain it for repairs."

With concurring smiles and laughter, they all piled back into Matte's SUV looking forward to the moment they would launch out on to the cool, deep water under the bright warm summer sky.

Chad was fiddling with Tess's camera and discussing his project with her as they pulled into Wahweap Marina where Matte kept his large pontoon boat. Glad to be at their destination, everyone scrambled to grab their provisions and make way to the boat. After an intense hour of securing their goods, checking the emergency gear and fueling up, they parted the waters of the marina and headed up the lake's main channel at full throttle. They planned to spend their first night at the lake on a small island out of Wahweap near Navajo Canyon. In order to have camp set up before dusk, they would need to move along. It was a perfect day, the weather was beautiful and as they raced along the surface of the gleaming water, everyone felt the exhilaration of being out in the fresh air in the middle of such breathtaking scenery. Chad snapped some pictures of them stowing in at the marina and now made notes in a log book and took more pictures as they cut through the water. Bright orange sandstone ledges were reflected in the brilliant, clear water; the ridge line creating a horizon dividing the infinite blue sky above from the deep water below. Tess took the binoculars and spotted an eagle perched on a craggy outcropping of rock and pointed it out to the boys. Soon they heard the eagles call and another majestic bird appeared, swooping down, gliding along the steep ledges. As Angie stepped to the helm and handed Matte a cup of coffee, she placed her arms around his waist and leaning in on his shoulder asking, "Does it get better than this?"

With a warm smile and a kiss to her forehead he replied, "No, it doesn't."

Their home for the night loomed up out of the water just ahead, the pinnacle of a single monolith, jutting straight up from what was once the canyon floor now made island by the surrounding waters, a partly submerged mesa only accessible to man by the flow of water around it. As they put in to tie up, the campers noted how the sun was waning and a quick supper would need to be prepared while the guys pitched the tent and hauled in the bed rolls. Later, seated comfortably around a camp fire with their tummies full of savory beef stew and biscuits, they sipped at mugs of spiced tea and marveled at the giant, full moon and plethora of stars and constellations that littered the night sky.

Bats began to dart out of holes grooved in the side walls of stone to begin their nocturnal feasting. Buzz-bombing the campfire, they screeched and flapped their webbed wings, then flew off into the silent night. Jordan teased his mom by hoping he could catch one in his fishing net and slip it into her bed roll for a surprise, which she assured him would only lead her to drown him at first light. Matte grinned at Jordan and told him a man who is forewarned is forearmed and they all laughed. While conversing around the flickering fire, Tess withdrew from her shirt pocket the small worn envelope she had found earlier in the day with her camera equipment. She passed the photos around explaining the images with the details of her life at that time. The two boys loved the old car and Angie commented on how young and spunky she and Max looked in those days. Matte loved seeing old pictures of his father, with whom he had enjoyed a close relationship. Tagging along behind him as a young boy, Matte was full of wonder as his father unveiled the splendors of nature to him and a love for God's great creative work. It filled him with a sense of pleasure. Chad asked about the bowl that Granddad held up in his hands and Tess explained about the ancient Anasazi Indians who produced this unique type of black and white pottery and the Pueblo people who were their late ancestors. She described this particular excavation trip was intended to yield fossils fragments and dinosaur bones and what an added bonus it had been to find these other items. As the fire drew to its dying embers, Chad stared at the picture of his granddad and the ancient bowl. He wondered who had made it and used it, and what life was like for that person who lived tucked away in the remote ledges of time.

For the next few days, operating from their base camp on the island, the family launched out on their boat to ride the gleaming still waters. They traveled up into remote eddies, that pierced the windswept sandstone ledges where they climbed up nearby rocks and dove off the lower cliffs, splashing and frolicking in the cool, deep water. Jordan, who loved to snorkel, adjusted his breathing tube and face mask as he jumped in and paddled several yards from the anchored pontoon; smoothly swimming along the surface until he spotted a school of fish. Then, hanging quietly in the water, suspended in a dead man's float, the fish came up to look in his face mask. They nibbled at his fingers and toes as they swam between his motionless limbs investigating this newcomer to their native waters. Through his mask, Jordan could see straight down for almost fifty feet through the shafts of light that broke the surface until shadows shrouded the cavernous bottom below. Grandma Tess began to make a list of the birds she sighted, drawing small doodled sketches by some just for fun. In the open channel leading up the Escalante River, they spent a lazy afternoon picnicking and fishing for their supper. By the time they headed back to their encampment in late afternoon, their ice chest was full of beautiful rainbow trout found to be plentiful in these waters. By the end of their fourth day it was time to revisit the marina for more fuel and some fresh provisions. This time they visited the Pawnee Marina, a more remote outpost near Goats Bluff on the western shore of Lake Powell.

As they pulled in to tie up near the main store, Matte decided Chad would go with the women to help them with their supplies and Jordan would assist him with the fuel and water needs. As Tess, Angie, and Chad made their way down the wharf toward the store, Chad noticed a few Indians going into the shop and an old one sitting outside its door on a small worn chair sleeping in the sun. With a face like a road map, lines ran all over his brown crinkled flesh and arched from the corners of his eyes like small waterfalls, making their way over his high cheekbones and into the sunken hallows on either side of his large bony nose. On his head sat an old black felt hat with a rawhide headband that held a white feather, its tip dipped in black. This ancient father was what some would call older than dirt and twice as dusty, as he sat there perfectly still in his faded blue jeans, worn cotton shirt and pointy-toed cowboy boots that had seen too many miles already. He held the look of a character from a western dime novel. Chad tried not to stare as he entered the store but was so taken with the man's appearance that he stumbled while stepping over the threshold. In a flash, the old man leapt from his chair and grabbed Chad's arm to break his fall. Startled by this action, Chad sucked in his breath and looked alarmed as he righted himself. Chad was further surprised when he looked up into the old man's face and noticed his milky white and brown eyes that no doubt compromised his vision, yet seemingly sharpened his other senses. Just as this happened, Tess turned around and saw the old Indian holding Chad's arm. She walked to the door to see what was going on. The old fellow released Chad and asked him if he was all right, grinning a broad toothless smile. Tess and Chad said yes and thanked the man as he went on to explain that his name was Jesse Billagoaty and that his son George owned this store and had hired him to be his watch dog. All three laughed, while Tess complimented him on a job well done.

For the next two hours, the family shopped and took time to have a cold lunch of sandwiches, potato salad and dill pickles found at a snack counter in the back of the store. Ice cold lemonade came from a large canister called "Pink Gully Washer." All imbibed and asked for more. As they finished up and readied for the boat, Chad wandered back outside where he engaged Mr. Billagoaty in conversation. Chad had pulled up a large stump of wood and sat next to Jesse asking him all sorts of questions about himself like how old he was, what kind of Indian tribe he came from and where he lived. Jesse was of a mind to converse and obliged his young friend with some colorful facts about his life, then had a few questions of his own. By the time the family came out of the store with their packages in hand, Chad and Jesse had become fast friends.

The sun hung low in the sky as the Harpers moved up the main channel of Lake Powell then on to the tributary leading to their camp. Chad kept the family entertained during the journey with facts about his new friend. Jesse Billagoaty revealed he was ninety-six years old and a member of the Navajo Indian Nation. He was born in 1915 on the land grant reservation in southern Utah just across the Utah-Arizona border. He grew up in a region called Comb Ridge, where his family subsisted on a bit of land they farmed and sheep his dad raised to sell and traded. As a boy, Jesse loved to run and play out in the sage brush that covered the rolling hills surrounding his home. He learned to snare rabbits, gather wild bird eggs and chew on pear cactus, that when the needles were shaved off, release a tangy natural juice. His favorite food was hoe cakes that his mother fried over an open fire in a cast iron skillet, made from corn meal with fresh onion and green pepper added in season. Jesse told Chad that at his age, he was put out to tend his father's sheep, gather firewood for his mother's cook stove, and to keep the weeds from overtaking their small garden. In the winter of his twelfth year, he had learned to read, being taught by Christian missionaries who had come to the reservation to spread the white man's gospel, handing out Bibles to all who would listen. In the comfort and knowledge of a great creative spirit was found a common theme used to reach the people in his village, many who did come to faith over time. Chad said he told Jesse about his granddad and the Indian bowl he had found. Jesse confirmed, based on its description, that it had no doubt come from the ancient ones and that his own mother had been skilled at braiding rugs and weaving, their patterns and techniques passed down from generation to generation. The family showed real interest in Chad's story and later that night by the camp fire light, he wrote about this wonderful chance meeting in his journal, happy that Jesse allowed his picture to be taken at their parting, should their paths never cross again.

Their time at the lake finally spent, had been refreshing and wonderful, all they had hoped for. Now as the Harpers' broke camp and stowed their gear on the pontoon, Jordan policed the area, checking for any leftover trash while Chad dispersed the campfire site and buried the ashes. Pushing off their moorings they pulled up the lines one last time and headed for Wahweap, then to the road that would lead home.

They made their final passage across the lake, reflecting on what a great trip it had been, the natural beauty of the area and the many things they had seen and done. Chad read parts of his journal out loud to include some antics that had happened around the campfire. They talked about the nights they had told stories, sung songs and laughed at each other while eating smores. How they loved that sticky marshmallow and chocolate smeared across their chins. They all agreed once again, it doesn't get better than this!

Once back in the SUV and heading up the grade leading to Page, they decided by unanimous vote to take a small detour down Highway 89 and over to Marble Canyon past Navajo Bridge. The family hadn't been that way in a few years and Tess told them some interesting facts about the area and the Pueblo Indians that had been traced to the Paria Plateau, a geographic location rich in Indian artifacts and history. When they entered the area, they found a lodge and four small shops connected by a boardwalk. The shops were laden with wonderful handmade Indian blankets, rugs, baskets, pottery, and more. Across the road and set back in a stand of Russian olive trees was an adobe building housing a rock shop, set against a high vertical cliff now left in shadow as the afternoon sun marched across the sky. In the shade of its porch was a sagging wooden bench where a man sat smoking his pipe, stroked a large and lazy fat cat. While the family explored the outpost, Tess decided to venture across the road to look at the rocks. As she made for the porch she glanced at the man and his cat and couldn't believe what she saw; there was Jessie Billagoaty staring forward out of his milky, brown, sightless eyes. Now detecting her footsteps, he turned his head in her direction, raised his eyebrows and smiled. Tess called out Jessie's name and reminded him of their meeting a few days past at the Pawnee Marina and the young lad he had kept from a fall. Jessie bobbed his head and laughed with the recollection. Tess shook her head and smiled as she asked Jessie how it was that he was now miles away from the lake and here at the Rock Shop at Paria Plateau. Jessie told Tess that his nephew, Little John ran the Rock Shop and they both said in unison, "And he hired me to be his watch dog!" Both laughed at the old man's joke.

As the two moved inside so Tess could explore, Jessie introduced Little John to his new friend and pleasantries were exchanged. Tess had learned quite a bit about rocks over the years while tagging along with Max on some of his expeditions and had developed a real appreciation for the beauty and mysteries of creation trapped in their form. As Tess strolled along the trestle tables that held the various specimens, Jessie remained at her elbow with an ongoing commentary about the stories and legacy of Mother Earth held and revealed in each unique kind of rock and that the rocks speak to those who know how to listen.

Little John approached Tess and announced he held in his hands a rare piece that possessed special qualities, Jessie sighed and called it *taheebo*, not to be confused with a tree bark of the same name. Jessie went on to explain that one special attribute the bark and rock shared however, is that both possess mystical properties for healing the body and soul. Jessie reached out for Tess's hand which she freely gave as he began to whisper in a reverent, conspiratorial voice, that this rock was quartz embedded with shards of crystal and flickers of golden Isinglass and that Indian legend tells how this particular rock formation holds the handprint of God, the great creator and that all who touch it can feel a special vibration reverberate from its own magnetic field.

Tess noticed that Jessie's blind eyes held a particular sparkle as he went on to detail for her that through the vibrations, the rock bears witness to man that what is bound on earth is also bound in heaven and that the very throne of God is replete with these same glowing, luminescent properties found in the *taheebo* rock; and that through its vibrations, the wholeness of God's love for the universe he created can be known.

Tess stood transfixed by the hypnotic message delivered in Jessie's hushed tones as Chad burst through the door of the rock shop and saddled up to his grandma's side, then in the exuberance of recognition, threw his arms around Jessie Billagoaty as he called out his name. The old father returned the boy's embrace as he laughed and smiled with affection. Amazement and wonder registered again on the second Harper in one day to encounter Jessie away from his customary perch on the porch at the marina. As the same explanation for Jessie's whereabouts was given once again, Tess introduced her grandson to Little John, and a brief update was shared with Chad concerning the facts about the *taheebo* rock. He was more than fascinated by this mysterious harbinger of God's whisper in man's ear. The sheer beauty of this idea that a supreme and loving God would choose to interact with man through the glory of his creation held them all motionless and spellbound. At that very moment of contemplation, sunshine pierced the windows of the shop and moved across the rock being held in Little John's hand as God-light shot through its multiple facets, bathing the room in a prism of swirling color. Jessie invited Tess and Chad to reach out and touch the rock, as his own long fingertips sought out the hand of God. Knowing glances were exchanged as something strange and wonderful happened. A presence bathed the heart of each one caught in the light and filled them with a whispering spirit that said, "Be still and know that I am."

The moment came and went. The small group huddled around the rock, holding its glowing body in one moment and then were standing in deep, silent shadow as the sun withdrew from the windows and slid behind the tree line ledges across the ravine. For several moments, no one moved or said a word, and then slowly Little John withdrew the rock and took it to a back room where it was kept. Jessie began to sway in a gentle rhythm and sing softly a song of praise in his native tongue, his frail arms reaching up and hands waving in adoration. Chad moved to the arms of his grandma Tess and they stood there holding each other, their moist eyes and joyful hearts were a testimony that something special was happening that neither would ever forget.

A bit later, Little John returned to flip the closed sign in his front window and hand out mugs of warm apple cider to his guests. The group settled into mismatched chairs in various stages of disrepair that were scattered throughout the shop. Tess used her cell phone to call Matte, who was comfortably ensconced at the lodge with Angie and Jordan. Tess informed him that she and Chad were fine and in the company of an old friend over at the rock shop and not to worry. Matte was fascinated to know the old Indian from the marina had family ties at Paria Plateau and chuckled at the irony of their seeing him again.

Lifting their mugs to enjoy the tangy sweetness of the cider, they relaxed and conversed about the Taheebo rock, its origins and where it had been found. Jessie told them a story about his grandfather whom they called Kehony, a name in their tradition that meant "spirit keeper." When Kehony was in his thirty-second year, he was part of an encampment of Navajos at a place called Cow Springs, on the north ridge of Black Mesa, halfway between what we now call Tuba City and Kayenta. He had gone out with a small hunting party to look for game one morning, when they emerged from a group of trees to find a deep gorge lined with unusual rock formations. Thick undergrowth choked the descent into this steep depression. The side walls of this place had small outcroppings of rock that caught the light and sparkled in the sun, while giving off a vibration, a powerful presence they all felt.

My grandfather knew this place was a holy place and he fell to his knees and could not move. Others in the party were fearful and scrambled back up the steep slopes to run away. As my grandfather's story has been told over the years, more questions than answers have been revealed as to what actually happened to him that day. Legend has it that he laid there on the ground for a long time speechless, watching celestial light dance and swirl across the ledges, glinting with sparkles of light that could be felt in his body. Overwhelmed with an intense sense of love and devotion, he cried out in unimaginable ecstasy, held in that moment. It was only after the sun fell behind a nearby plateau that grandfather felt the presence retreat, leaving him emotionally spent and physically weak. As the last rays of the dying sun washed the desert floor, Kehony crawled from the gorge and later entered the camp holding the Taheebo rock. Members of the hunting party rushed out to greet him saying they thought he might be dead and were anxious to hear about his experience. Around the communal fire that night, as all gathered to hear the tail, Kehony spoke of the great spirit of creation that is in all things and how the rocks spoke to him and blessed him with their sacred knowledge. He showed them the Taheebo, the healing rock, and all agreed it was true destiny that Kehony had been named spirit keeper at his birth, perhaps for just such a moment as this.

Tess and Chad hung on every word of Jessie's story, a tale that Little John had heard many times before. Tess finally asked Jessie if he had ever been to the mysterious gorge with its shining rock formations. He admitted that over the years he had done some exploring, but never happen upon the right location. Tess's eyebrows arched as an expression of glee lit her face.

"Jessie, would you like to find it if you could?" Tess asked.

The old man's face became animated and Little John leaned in to hear what Tess would say next.

She went on to explain that there were now finely tuned instruments able to detect a broad spectrum of geological elements as well as vibration frequencies at virtually any geographic location, and that they are the stock and trade of most professional geologists. At this point, Chad excitedly chimed in to say he knew his granddad had those kinds of instruments because his dad showed them to him a few years ago, when they were out in the shop behind Tess's house.

"That's right," said Tess. Jessie began to laugh as Little John sat staring at Tess while smiling and shaking his head.

He then said, "Are you suggesting we go out there and look for this place with your instruments?"

Tess and Chad looked at each other and grinned as Tess said, "Yes!"

Over the next week, plans were discussed among the Harper and Billagoaty families as to when and where to begin the search. Matte and Jordan were fascinated with the idea of an excursion, after seeing the stone with its unusual properties and hearing the circumstances of its origin. Matte had six days left of his vacation and thought an adventure off in the wild with his boys could be fun, and of course, Tess would keep things lively with her ambitions for prospecting. Tess would handle the technical supplies, Matte and the boys organized the tools and necessary hardware while the Billagoaty's provided maps and a list of landmark coordinates, long preserved among family members, and some camping provisions. They decided to rendezvous at the Rock Shop in two days at 8:00 a.m. and head northeast up Highway 160 to the Cow Springs area and to what they hoped would be the answer to an age-long mystery.

When they arrived in Cow Springs, it amounted to a wide spot in the road with a few farm houses, a gas station, and general store that supplied basic needs: from string and nails to canned spaghetti. Jessie and Tess entered the store while Little John and Matte filled the SUV and Little John's truck with gas. The boys looked for a spigot in case more water was needed later on. Tess asked a portly man behind the counter which road would be best to take to explore the north region of Black Mesa as she put her map on the counter and reached for some matches.

The man behind the counter eyed the two old folks in front of him with a curious grin, and asked why on earth they would want to head out there. He said it was a remote desert area and unforgiving in the summer heat. He then laughed out loud as he suggested they would be better off to stay on the beaten path, no pun intended. Tess arched her left brow, with a look of condescension on her face, and asked if the Hickiwan Road was still open, or had it been washed out by the severe spring rains this year.

Convinced the old woman and her Indian sidekick were serious and determined, he took a look at the map and said Topawa road would be a better choice because the forestry service had gone in to do some conservation and had graded the road to where it dead ends at Chaney's Point.

Tess gave the man her warmest smile and thanked him, then whirled around and sighed, and made for the door while Jessie paid for the matches, then fell in behind. Back at the vehicles they spread the map out again and discussed their options. Little John said as far as he could tell, Topawa would put them in closer to where the old riverbed lines up with Cedar Glenn where they should make camp and begin to explore. So it was decided, thirteen miles up the road from Cow Springs they would take a left on Topawa and cut down through the swells of rolling hills clustered with cedar trees. They traveled over red clay and sandy ribbons of road that led them along windswept gullies, where dust devils danced among the blue sage.

It was mid-afternoon when Jessie and Little John agreed they were about where they should be to secure a base camp and test out their equipment. On a low ridge, dotted with wild cedar and scrub oak that overlooked a dried riverbed some 100 yards ahead, they pulled off the road and into a small clearing. From their position on a modest rise of land, they could see off in the distance in several directions. Tess grabbed her field glasses and followed the contours of the land in a complete circle, describing various landmarks they could use as coordinates in the days ahead. Chad sat on a camp stool beside his grandma and wrote down the details she noted. By the time camp was set up and a quick bite of food was eaten as they worked, the sun had drifted behind the cliffs to the west. Sitting around the campfire later that night, they looked over their maps under a lantern hung on a pole. Jessie once more spoke of his Indian traditions and his grandfather who had enjoyed the love and respect of his people because of the example he had set throughout his life, the way he reverenced the land, and how he was filled with gratitude for all the abundant resources with which God had blessed his people.

As the sparks from the fire rose into the air then vanished in the darkened night sky, the full moon's large glowing orb rose over the mountain top and sailed on a tide of slow-moving clouds that stretched over the mesa, bathing the dramatic landscape in ghostly twilight. In the distance, the coyotes' call could be heard, their whimpers and whines from the bluffs beyond. While each in turn said his good nights,

Jessie remained by the fire humming a chant he learned as a boy and wandered if he himself would soon walk in the footsteps of his ancient father the spirit keeper.

For the next two days, the search party fanned out from their base camp to see what they could find. They broke up the canvassed area into quadrants as they walked from the center of camp and marked the coordinates Tess had noted. Reviewing the list of sketchy clues they had from Jessie's family lore and their limited knowledge of the area, they only hoped this mysterious place still existed. On the morning of the third day, as they filled their backpacks and readied for their walk, they discussed what had been seen so far and talked about what direction should be taken now. Matt suggested that as they had spent two days in the northern, eastern, and western quads, why not try the southern? All agreed it was time to look south.

As the sun climbed high in the sky, clouds offered relief shielding the hikers from the intense sun and a slight breeze moved in from the northwest. One could smell the promise of rain in the air. After lunch and a short rest, the party moved on down through the foothills and again came in contact with the meandering dry riverbed that only flowed with water during the spring runoff. Just over the dry bed was another large run of cedars and scrub oaks so the group spread out walking toward the trees.

Jessie was humming as he walked behind Little John to whom he was tethered. The wind soon kicked up and out in the distance a boom of thunder rolled in across the plateau. All of the sudden, Jessie began to chant in a loud voice, alarming Little John who now looked at his uncle in surprise. Then a holler from Jordan indicated he was getting a reading of vibrations on his instrument. Tess, who was nearby, thought it might be caused by the thunder and called for Jordan to check it again. Next, Matte yelled that he felt rain and pointed out an impression in a hillside up in front of him. He said for all to head that way to ride out the storm.

As the small group collected their gear and huddled together in the shallow cave, the heavens broke loose and poured down rain in a might torrent. Lightning flashed and more thunder roared over the dry scorched desert. Jessie said he felt something as they moved through the trees earlier and that the feeling was getting stronger when the rain came down. Jordan concurred, saying it was when he moved through the trees that his meter started to make a signal. After a thirty-minute downpour, the dark brooding clouds began to pass over the valley and the sun peeked through here and there producing a spectacular patchwork of light and shadow on the refreshed and drenched landscape; filling the air with the pungent fragrance of blue sage.

Heading back toward the thicket of trees from the backside this time, the group tried to reposition themselves where they had been before the storm, when Jessie called the group to a halt. Putting his hands up in the air, his blind eyes staring heavenward, he murmured to himself for a moment or two, then told the group he felt something, a tingling sensation and he grabbed for Little John's arm to support himself as he slowly inched forward in the direction of the vibration. The entire group was fascinated by this turn of events and excited at the prospect that they might have found the source of the Taheebo rock. Next, the group coalesced tightly around Jessie and moved forward at a snail's pace searching carefully for any depressions in the ground as they pushed away branches and brush in their path. Within minutes Jordan's meter began a slow beep-beep and its red indicator light switched on, pulsing with the beeping signal.

The party pushed away at the dense lush foliage now sopped and glistening with water. Tess stepped forward once more and suddenly slid down an incline through a mop of soggy wet branches and short bushy shrubs, letting out a terrifying yelp while caught off guard and falling. Matte instantly called to his mother, and flew in after her, the rest in turn followed suit. Once they were all accounted for at the bottom of the small ravine, they took stock of themselves and began to survey their surroundings. From what they could tell, they had fallen at least twenty-five feet along a forty-five-degree decline and landed at the base of a shallow pit. All around them they saw sandstone walls with bits of scrub oak precariously clinging to the ledges with shallow tough roots. They all noted a pulsation in the air they could both hear and feel. Jordan's meter gave off a continuous sound now and its red light held steady. Jordan switched it off.

As they began to move about and explore the pit, the sun that danced in and out of the clouds after the storm, now pierced the sky over the tree tops and hit the side walls of the pit with a miraculous, startling glow. Darkened recesses in the walls were now luminescent and literally sparkled like gleaming gems that had initially gone unseen in the deep wet shadows of the sand stone. The sun light coming just as it did that day in the Rock Shop, once again revealed the dazzling brilliance of these few rare outcroppings stuck in the walls. They all stared wide-eyed in fascination, when all of the sudden the ground shook and a rumbling sound reverberated off the ravine walls sending Jessie and Tess tumbling to the ground. Jessie, while on his knees, began to rhythmically chant and Matte ran to his mother to lift her to her feet. Jessie then motioned to the others to gather in a circle and bow down, for they were trampling on sacred ground, and as they did this the ground shook violently again and a chunk of Taheebo stone fell from the south wall of the pit and bounced across the ground landing near the group. With all that was happening, suddenly there was a great whooshing sound, as a fierce gust of wind whirled over the top of the pit, hovered a moment, then vanished as quickly as it had come. The sun that had shown so brilliantly just moments before now moved behind the straggling clouds and all was still and silent.

Stunned and gasping for breath, the small huddle of humans at the bottom of the pit were not sure what had just happened; they exchanged glances but were too amazed to utter a word. All were transfixed by a strong presence of power they all felt. For the next several minutes they stood quietly, each one reflecting on that moment of awe and wandering what might happen next. After some time passed, Tess cautiously lifted her head to look around. Her eyes darted across the ravine's expanse to see where the Taheebo rock had been dislodged from the south wall. Chad followed her eyes and then saw what she saw.

There in the crevice where the rock had been held, was another portion of Flag Stone protruding out of the wall that had some sort of markings scored on its face. Slowly, Tess and Chad left the huddle and crept to the wall for a closer look. Matte watched them and soon came up beside Chad, and taking a small hand pick from his belt, began to chisel around the stone. In a moment or two, it was freed and Matte gently lowered it down to the ground where all gathered around to investigate its markings. The stone itself was about twelve inches high and sixteen inches long. Tess said there appeared to be some sort of ancient writing on the stone and noted the design of a figure etched in the center of what looked like text.

Jessie said that tradition held there was a special cult within the Anasazi nation whose written form of communication at one time was used exclusively for worship purposes. Chad asked if the figure in the center of the rock was to represent God.

Tess ruffled his hair and said, "That could very well be its meaning."

Tess then suggested what they were looking at might even be some kind of American Indian Rosetta Stone holding the mysteries of worship by the ancient ones in this holy place, and they all smiled at the prospect. It was now early evening and the explorers knew they must move to be back in camp by night fall. As the Taheebo rock sample was carefully wrapped and placed in a backpack by Jordan, while Tess and Matte formed a sling out of Matte's extra jacket, to pull the etched Flag Stone back to camp. The waning sun set the surrounding cliffs on fire while the sky deepened to a steel azure blue, a pale circle of moon only a promise. The group crawled from the ravine and set their compass for base camp.

Late into the night they sat around their campfire going over again and again the extraordinary events of the day. They could not believe how lucky they had been to locate the actual spot in the desert they were looking for. What were the chances? They continued to examine the two rock samples they brought back. Jessie told the group that when he first met Chad and Tess he felt a special connection toward these two perfect strangers and then upon meeting them again felt it was fate. God had intended all along for them to become friends and find his secret hidden place.

They continued to examine and discuss the two rock samples with intensity. Soon, the significance of their find began to register on them. These two specimens they possessed were indeed rare and the inscribed sand stone in particular would have great intrinsic value as a link to the ancient Anasazi civilization of the Four Corners basin. Many in the academic world and the public at large would be fascinated and interested in their discovery. Tess pondered all of this as she curled up in her sleeping bag that night, reviewing in her mind, who was left on her personal and professional contact list that could help them decipher the unusual writing on the rock.

Back in Cow Springs the next day, the prospectors gassed up their vehicles at the general store and formulated a plan for what should come next. Tess and Matte decided to take possession of the rocks so that Tess could contact an old colleague at the University of Utah, Dr. Samuel Reese, a director of field studies in the anthropology department. He was a well-known expert on Western Indian Antiquities, and might be able to help solve the code.

The group made plans to stay in contact through the Rock Shop at Paria Plateau. Little John, Tess and Matte exchanged cell phone numbers and pledged to talk at least once a week so all could stay informed. Jessie said he had an old friend whose father had been a Navajo Medicine man and knew much about the old religious ceremonies and traditions. He might be able to reveal clues concerning the inscription on the Flag Stone, and Jesse suggested they contact him in the days to follow. With hugs and handshakes all around, the group split up and drove off, each heading for their individual homes, excited to solve the next phase of the mystery. Jessie had always claimed that rocks could talk to those who knew how to listen, and now the group was convinced they possessed one that was dying to tell its story.

Dr. Samuel Reese was an affable man with a ready smile and inquisitive keen eyes, who when asked, would unabashedly admit that his idea of creature comforts was to find himself quietly sitting among dusty relics and piles of old bones. After he opened the door to his private study, being alerted by his secretary that Tess Harper had arrived, he walked into the outer office with arms extended to greet his old friend whom he hadn't seen in a decade. Had it not been for the Christmas cards, he would have lost track of her entirely. As the two friends embraced, the years melted away and they found themselves engaged in the usual banter of colleagues who had shared many good jokes and tall tales over the years. Laughing with the pleasure of renewed friendship, Samuel ushered Tess back into his study and offered her a seat near the window and a steaming cup of coffee, which she readily accepted on this cool, rainy September morning. Settling into a leather wing chair beside her, Samuel commented on how good Tess looked and how wonderful it was to see her again. Then with a conspiratorial smirk on his face and raised eyebrows, he asked Tess about the unsolved mystery she had mentioned over the phone; something about a rock she had found. He made himself comfortable with a foot stool while reaching for his coffee and became more intrigued by the sparkle in Tess's eyes.

Tess began by telling Samuel of her trip to Lake Powell with her family in August, and how meeting the old Indian named Jessie Billagoaty started a whole string of events that led to the discovery of the Taheebo Rock and the inscribed Flagstone. Tess reached into her shoulder bag and removed a folder containing several photographs of the two rocks. She handed them to Samuel, who took his reading glasses from the top of his head where they had been nesting on his bald spot, and adjusted them at the end of his nose.

Putting down his coffee mug, he leaned over the photos for a closer look. Several minutes later, he settled back in his chair and said that this was all very interesting and verified with Tess that these samples had indeed come from the south side of Black Mesa. Tess concurred. Samuel shared with Tess that two years ago, he had led a group on a dig at Black Mesa, but their search of the ground on the western bench revealed nothing of real significance. Samuel, surveying his memory said he had seen similar markings like the one on the Flagstone only once before, on a tribal chieftain's breastplate dating back to the Anasazi period that had been cataloged at around 740 B.C. Dr. Reese said that it had come from the Herrington Edwards project near Vermillion Cliffs out of Escalante in 1983. Samuel said he remembered this because the project yielded such a large cash of artifacts.

Then walking to his desk, he buzzed his secretary and asked her to check the archives for any film or still photos from that project. Tess was intrigued by Samuel's input and hoped she might get a glimpse of the breastplate to compare its writing. While they were waiting, Samuel asked Tess where the rocks were being stored. She replied that they were in Max's old lab behind her home in Red Mesa. He said he would love to see the rocks, for then he could better investigate their significance, especially if they could find a correlation between the texts of both artifacts. Samuel and Tess exchanged knowing glances at one another, as Tess webbed her fingers together on her chin. She settled back in her chair in deep thought and gazed out the window at the rain drizzling down the window pane.

As the two finished their coffee, there came a knock on the study door, and Samuel's intern Jeff Hodges handed Samuel a folder marked Vermillion Cliffs Section 143-83. Tess stood to stretch as she moved toward the small conference table at the end of the room where Samuel was spreading out eight-by-ten black and white photos. Picking up his magnifying glass, Samuel held up the first photo and scrutinized the details on the breast plate. Sharp vertical lines formed the characters with occasional intersecting, short straight lines at a right or left angel in multiples of two or three. A short barb was found at the end of the vertical lines with three strokes to the left.

"A very simplistic type of cuneiform originating along the banks of the Euphrates river valley in the Middle East would be a good comparison," Samuel said as he handed the photo and glass to Tess.

She was fascinated with the writing on the breast plate and went to retrieve the Taheebo rock pictures she left sitting near her chair.

The two colleagues bent over the table and carefully studied the characters on the breastplate, comparing it with the rock and to their delight they were quite similar, the exception being the addition of some small dot like features on the rock.

"Has anyone ever tried to make an interpretation from the breastplate?" asked Tess.

"There hasn't been anything published in an official way, but I know there have been some theories discussed," said Samuel. "Dr. Halbertt over at the language lab was called in as a consultant when the relic was discovered; you might want to talk with him," he continued.

Samuel told Tess that Halbertt thought the breast plate writing had religious significance with what looked to be a reference to deity and a great spirit.

"What did he base his opinion on?" Tess asked.

Samuel commented that Halbertt claimed some segments of the early hieroglyphics and cuneiform samples from the same period have corresponding markings and speak of similar religious concepts. Tess said she would love to speak with Dr. Halbertt. Samuel said he would be happy to set up a meeting and asked how he could get in touch with her while she was in Salt Lake City. Tess gave him her cell phone number and said she would be at the Hilton for the next three days, while she put on her jacket and grabbed her file and placed it back in her bag. Walking Tess to the door, Samuel once again took Tess's hand in his own and shook it with affection saying he would be in touch and bid her farewell.

The next afternoon, Tess received a call from Samuel who had arranged a meeting with Dr. Halbertt for 5:00 p.m. at his lab at the university, located at Smith Hall on the north side of campus. When Tess arrived, she was warmly greeted by the two professors. Samuel had the black and whites of the breastplate out on a table that was placed in the center of the room, illuminated by a large florescent light. Tess reached for her file on the rocks and joined them. Dr. Halbertt smiled at Tess and told her he had always been amazed and intrigued at how the relics of the past whisper to us down through the centuries as a testimony of our own ongoing humanity, each age encapsulating the history of its moment in time. Tess smiled back at Dr. Halbertt and told him he had the soul of a poet and they all laughed as they then turned their attention to the photos. Dr. Halbertt said after his conversation with Samuel, he took the liberty of assembling some comparative samples of cuneiform and hieroglyphics on which he based his original observations concerning the breast plate.

As the three bent over the samples, Dr. Halbertt proceeded to point out the characters known to speak of God and a great spirit of creation. Tess pointed with her fingers from one sample to another as she picked up on the repetitions and became excited. She then asked Dr. Halbertt what he thought of the etched figure in the middle of the Flagstone. Looking closer with his magnifier, he said it had human features though somewhat distorted, then as he moved the glass further from the photo he said the words, "God with us."

Tess said, "What did you say?"

Dr. Halbertt told them that in very small characters, around the neck of this central figure, in what at first glance seems to be simple ornamentation, is actually text that says "God with us" and if you are careful to examine the text, he went on, you will begin to see that apart from the writing at perfectly symmetrical intervals there are rays emanating from the figure who must represent God.

The group fell silent as they took some time to ponder this information. It was ultimately decided that both the Taheebo rock that emitted measurable energy and the inscribed Flagstone were extremely important finds and should be documented and housed in the University Museum of Indigenous Peoples in Salt Lake City. Plans were made to have the rocks moved to the museum. Tess prepared a full report to the curator that would accompany the two remarkable rocks to their new home.

A public showing was being scheduled for the middle of November, with a full-page story in the Salt Lake Tribune documenting the discovery. A reporter from the Trib traveled to Red Mesa to interview the family about their adventure at Lake Powell and their inadvertent involvement in solving the mystery of an ancient Indian legend.

The opening of the exhibit was truly a thrilling event. The entire Harper family was in attendance as was Little John and Jessie Billagoaty, who soon became the star of the show. Jessie dressed to the nines for the auspicious occasion by sporting a new pair of Levi's with a black dress coat and a pair of shiny new boots bought for him by Little John. His white hair was swept back under his old felt hat with the feather on it. The finishing touch was his snake skin bolo tie with silver hand-tooled tassels at each end. Jessie was full of smiles and gladly shook hands to greet all who had questions for him and seemed to enjoy all the hub-bub. Later that evening, as the excitement was coming to an end, Jessie shared that he had visited with his friend whose father had been a medicine man. He had knowledge of stories about the ancient ones having encounters with the creator, who had taught the people secrets of spiritual wisdom, and that they had written this information on rocks for posterity. Tess embraced Jessie and said he was so right about the rocks ability to speak to those who choose to listen and how man is without excuse, to know and understand from all that has been created, that there is one truly powerful God.

Chad, who was so excited to see the pictorial display of his photos of the Lake Powell trip on display, decided one more was in order to bring their family saga to a close. Dr. Samuel Reese stepped forward and took hold of Tess's old Pentax camera and shot a picture of the Harper family, Little John and Jessie standing in front of the sacred rock display in the museum. Finally, as goodbyes were said at their parting, hugs and warm embraces were readily shared by the Harpers, Jessie and Little John. Tess took Jessie's old worn hands into her own and with emotion brimming in her eyes said to him, "Godspeed my friend," and in a gentle whisper he replied, "I will see you on the other side."

How much can one person lose in life and still remember who they are? Altered by tragedy but not destroyed, Asher Levy forged on, never giving up and never giving in to discouragement and his fragile, frayed, emotions. Then one morning fate stepped into the balance and changed his life forever. He would never think of life, death, or God in the same way again. Learn what Asher discovered about the mystery of our existence in **Seasons of the Heart.**

SEASONS OF THE HEART

Asher Levy never saw it coming that clear beautiful day in May, with such a bright blue sky that it almost put a spring in his step. As he walked from his home to his car, he planned what he would say to his boss that morning concerning the details of the merger he was working on. Asher had been an insurance executive for one of the larger companies in town for over twelve years and had finally achieved that coveted corner office on the fifth floor that overlooked Ralston Park. His administrative assistant, Laura Jacobs, was a genial woman with a commanding skill set that made his job easy. Yes, God had blessed Asher over the years as he climbed the corporate ladder and he had always felt his guiding presence with a sense of gratitude and praise.

As he entered the lobby of the Regent Building that morning where his office was located and headed for the elevator, he noticed a very distinguished looking man in an impeccably tailored, dark blue suit with shiny, silver hair and neatly trimmed matching mustache. The man held in his right hand a beautiful oxblood leather attaché case and had a calm but purposeful look on his face. As Asher stepped closer to the elevator, he gave a slight nod and smiled to the man who returned his greeting in kind. The two men then entered the elevator together and began their assent to the fifth floor where both were apparently headed that morning.

During the elevator's upward climb, the two men alone in the compartment stared straight ahead in silence until there was a sudden jolt and a blink of the elevator's interior lights. There between the third and fourth floors, the indicators on the modular key panel lit up and then went dark as the compartment came to a grinding halt. While it became apparent that they were suspended between floors, the two men looked at one another: Asher in a state of surprise, the elegant gentleman with a quizzical smile and a slight glint in his eye.

With a nervous laugh Asher exclaimed, "Well this is a first," and he reached for the emergency phone on the wall.

As he anxiously spoke into the receiver, he soon realized that the phone was dead also and turned to face the other man, while gesturing with both hands that the phone was a no-go.

Asher slowly hung up the receiver while wondering what to do next. Finally, turning to look at his companion, he was further startled by the fact that there was now a radiant glow emanating from the man's figure. Wide-eyed at this surreal happening, Asher could not speak and just stood there looking on, transfixed in the moment. Then in a soft but powerful voice like a rushing wind, the man spoke to Asher in a way that seared his conscience and pierced his very soul.

The man asked, "Asher Levy, do you believe in divine destiny?"

Astounded by the realization of what seemed to be happening, some kind of angelic encounter that was intended specifically for him, Asher struggled to find his voice and words to respond to this presence. In a trembling, humbled way he finally uttered that he did believe that God has a purpose for all people and that he was grateful for God's presence in his life. The man then held out the case in his hand and told Asher to take it. He went on to explain that God had a special invitation for him and that he would find instructions inside the case. As Asher reached out and took hold of the case, the man instantly disappeared before his eyes and the elevator began to move upward again toward the fifth floor. Soon the door opened and Asher stepped out into the normal daily rush going on in the executive suite.

Feeling stunned by this strange experience, Asher quickly darted to his office where he entered, then closed the door behind him and went directly to sit in his desk chair, all the while clutching the briefcase to his chest. Several moments passed before he felt his heartbeat normalize and his breathing steady and even again. Still astonished, he slowly swiveled in his chair and looked out the window as he did most mornings, but this time the familiar scene seemed slightly skewed, or altered. Had he really just had this strange experience, or was he dreaming? Soon the rational side of his brain came to life and he realized he had actually arrived at his office and that he was indeed holding a briefcase that was not his own. As he sat there mystified, he drummed his fingers on the side of the case, trying to find the bravado to open it and peek inside.

Just as Asher pushed the release button on the case, there was a tap on the door, then Laura appeared with a blue file folder tucked under her arm and a cup of black coffee in her hand.

"Good morning," she said as she made her way to his desk, then laid the file down and handed him the coffee.

Laura took one look at Asher and asked if everything was all right, for he seemed a bit pale and shaky. He immediately placed the briefcase under his desk in the key hole and tried to flash her a casual, congenial smile while he reached for the file.

"All is well," he assured her "and thanks for the coffee," he said, "It always helps to get things going." Laura cocked her head to one side and stared at him, not fully convinced by what he said, but deferred to do further investigation, as he pointed to the papers in the blue folder and began asking questions.

Asher's day was fast-paced between meetings, conference calls and the routine shuffle of paper work. It was 6:00 p.m. before he leaned back in his chair and stretched his arms up over his head with a deep sigh, and decided to call it a day. Intermittently throughout the day, he had been drawn back into the memory of what happened that morning in the elevator but was still unable to process his thoughts in any meaningful way, or to look inside the case, due to the demands of his schedule.

As he now reached for his jacket and turned off his lamp, he noticed the briefcase in the key hole of his desk and was awash with anxiety once again as he bent down to pick it up. When he exited the office, he saw Laura gathering her purse and keys to go home and told her good night. She smiled and complimented him on his new briefcase and headed down the main hall that led to the elevator. Asher, having been tied to his desk most of the day, decided to take the stairs to get a little exercise, denying subconsciously that he was not ready for another elevator ride just yet.

Arriving home, Asher tossed his keys on the hall table and placed the day's mail beside them. He then went directly to the kitchen where he placed the briefcase on the counter and turned to the refrigerator to get some juice. Standing there in the half-light of early evening, he braced himself against the counter and drank deeply with satisfaction. As he drank, he looked at the briefcase and rehearsed the events of the elevator ride; still second guessing himself about the man he met and his instructions. Taking his glass of juice and the briefcase into the living room, he sat on the sofa and pondered why something like this would happen to a man like him.

Asher Levy was forty-two years old and a widower with no children. He and his wife Katherine had tried to have a family for many years but with no success. There was the heartbreak of three miscarriages and then Katherine became ill and died of leukemia when she was only thirty-eight years old and Asher was thirty-nine. The deep, crushing sadness he had experienced with those heavy losses could have easily destroyed him and would have taken down lesser men; but with each blow he found himself on his knees seeking God for comfort and answers, the kind of answers that often remain elusive this side of the heaven.

He had met Katherine while she was doing an internship with an architectural firm and he was fresh out of college looking to establish himself in business. He first saw her when he bumped into a mutual friend of theirs out for a late lunch at a local restaurant one afternoon. She was one in a party of five, noshing away at a blooming onion and a pile of curly fries. Her crooked smile and dimples were the first things to catch his eye and then as she spoke, he loved her light-hearted laughter and easy conversational style that seemed so natural. She was young, vivacious and full of life and he found her joy and optimism to be contagious. Oh, how he missed her still and the little ones they dreamed of scampering around that might have been.

Somehow over time, he had managed to make peace with their silent, cavernous house and not to bleed emotionally every time he ran into one of Katherine's personal possessions that he had failed to put away. Life had not turned out the way it had been planned, but Asher believed in redemption and refused to succumb to his darker emotions. He knew in his heart that despite all that had happened over the years, God was not through with him yet and that as long as he had breath, there was always hope for a new day. He recalled the best advice he had received from a friend at the time of Katherine's death, it was to keep on living until he felt like living again. He had pushed forward, opting for life, even on the days he was so numb he could barely feed himself.

Asher put his juice glass down on the coffee table and reached for the briefcase. With a deep sigh he pushed the clasp and opened the case. There inside was a single sheet of thick, creamy colored, parchment with a scripted message in black ink. Asher drew the paper out and looked at the beautiful calligraphy and began to read the words.

Asher Levy, you have an appointment tomorrow Tuesday, May 7, at 7:00 p.m. with a person named Christopher. Go to 707 Wayfair Street, then to apartment No. 17. Ask for Christopher, he will be there waiting for you. Take this message and the briefcase with you.

That was all it said. Asher fell back onto the sofa, his mind reeling, more perplexed than ever. Asher was curious about all of the sevens used in the day, time and address.

Determined to get a handle on this mystery, Asher went to the computer in his study and pulled up a map of the city and looked for Wayfair Street. He was unfamiliar with the name but soon found it listed on the fringes of a warehouse district near an industrial park. That seemed odd, for there weren't any inhabitable apartments in that section of town. He then tried to glean further information by entering that specific address into his search and came up with absolutely nothing. Leaning back in his chair, he stared at the monitor, wondering who this Christopher could be and why he needed to see him.

That night was spent in fitful bouts of tossing and turning intertwined with memories of the man in the blue suit handing him the briefcase, repeated episodes of the elevator's blinking lights and the compartment lurching up and down to the fifth floor. Totally exhausted the next morning from a lack of sleep, Asher arose from his bed still questioning himself about the entire situation but more intent than ever to get to the bottom of things. He also noticed that in spite of these strange circumstances, for some odd reason he felt a calming assurance down deep inside that everything was going to be alright.

The next day passed in the usual way. Laura had been in and out of Asher's office all morning long with papers for him to review and reminders from her appointment book concerning meetings and his power lunch with a new client at 1:00 p.m. at the Palms restaurant over on Hampton Street. Asher had really relied on Laura after Katherine's death to help him hold it in the road and march on. Her kindness and efficiency had been key to his ongoing success at the firm and he was so grateful for her friendship and professionalism. When the day ended, Asher was full of anxiety and anticipation as he drove across town to locate Wayfair Street. He wished there was someone he could share all of this with, someone to use as a sounding board but until he himself understood what was happening, he felt compelled to go it alone for now.

As he rounded a corner and spotted the street sign, he felt a slight lump in his throat. The area was a bit shabby and not well lit. Moving along the street slowly while searching for the number, he finally pulled up to the curb in front of a dark gray rundown warehouse flanked by overflowing trash cans on either side of its entrance. The number 707 scrawled unevenly in chipped black paint glared at him. This was the place. He sat in his car for a few moments, checking his watch and fidgeting with the briefcase that sat beside him. He had no idea what was about to happen but he felt compelled to move toward it never the less. Entering the front door, he stepped into a long, dimly lit hallway with concrete floors and marred metal doors some rusting. Asher noticed that the numbers on the doors inside were in the same irregular, chipped condition as the numbers on the front of the building. Locating No. 17, Asher quickly checked his watch and then gently knocked on the door. What happened next was so surprising that Asher had a hard time taking it in.

A small, wide-eyed, freckle-faced girl around the age of six or seven answered the door. She looked up at Asher through the glowing orb that was her face, and smiled a happy, toothless grin. Her two front teeth had fallen out and might have been exchanged for pixie dust and two quarters placed under a pillow.

"Hello," said Asher, explaining who he was and that he was there to see Christopher.

"Oh yes," the girl said. "He has been waiting for you," and she swung the door open and stepped aside so Asher could enter.

As he moved over the threshold, Asher was instantly mesmerized by the opulent interior; it was such a contrast to the exterior of the building and the cold, dark dingy hallway. He felt like he had actually entered another world.

Asher followed the small girl through a foyer where there were beautiful furnishings and fresh cut flowers, their sweet fragrance scenting the air. There was soft, dreamy music playing in the background. They walked along a marble floor, then onto a beautiful Persian rug accented with golden threads. The walls were a pale blush of yellow, trimmed in white and a dazzling, crystal chandelier was suspended from the ceiling that was painted with clouds and a sky that seemed to be moving. At the end of this hall stood two French doors, their glass panels etched with palm leaves and exotic birds. The small girl turned to Asher and requested the briefcase and parchment, then told him to wait there. She then turned one of the ornate gold doorknobs and disappeared between the doors.

In a matter of moments, the door opened again and there stood another child, this time a blond-headed blue-eyed boy of seven. He looked up at Asher, and instantly a wide smile lit his face while he reached out and took one of Asher's hands and led him inside. The space he stepped into was a covered patio, which led to an expansive, lush tropical garden. There were beautiful hanging plants and a path that led from the patio across a deep green lawn to a stone bridge that crossed over a shimmering pond flanked by soaring cyprus trees and weeping willows. There were wonderful birds and butterflies and every living thing around them buzzed with the palpable energy of life. The small lad guided Asher to a bench beneath a large blooming magnolia tree and patted the seat telling Asher to sit.

Again, the small boy beamed up at Asher and said, "Hi, I'm Christopher."

Asher sat there not knowing what to think as he looked around this fabulous, glistening paradise he had entered. Then glancing at Christopher in wonder, he said, "How is it, young man, that I have been invited here to meet you in this remarkable place, behind shabby, steel gray doors?"

Christopher then touched Asher's knee and said, "I have wanted to meet you for so long. I have watched you now and then and wished I could be with you, especially when you are sad and missing mom."

"Mom—" said Asher.

"What do you mean, Mom?" Asher asked.

"Katherine," said Christopher. Asher shook his head that was now dizzy with confusion and the pain of remembered loss.

"My Katie is your mom?" asked Asher.

Christopher then moved even closer to Asher and said, "That's right."

"I really don't understand what is going on here, is this some kind of bad joke?" Asher replied.

At this point something totally unexpected happened. Christopher got up from the bench and placed himself on his knees before Asher and took both of Asher's hands into his own, then through a supernatural glowing face he said to him, "I am the first baby you and Katherine lost, remember, you were going to name me Christopher?"

Asher sat there staring at the boy half with longing and half with disbelief. "I don't understand any of this," he said, "How can this be?"

Christopher told him that they were in a special place God had for children like him, who for one reason or another were unable to be brought into the fullness of life and that until God brings all things to their perfection he would shelter the little ones here.

"Would you like to see Sarah and Amy?" Christopher asked.

"My other two babies?" said Asher.

"Yes, I can take you to a place where you can watch them play; they love to dig in the sand," said Christopher.

Over a slight hill they looked down onto a play area with a sandbox where two glowing, curly headed, little girls giggled and chattered as they scooped sand from a brightly colored bucket and filled the plates and cups of a toy dish set. Asher's heart melted and he smile with the warmth and desire of a loving father.

Christopher told Asher that Katherine often comes to see them and they are filled with unspeakable joy when she wraps her arms around them and holds them close. He went on to say that eventually they would all be together in time, and that God in his great love and mercy for Asher, had let him take this peek into glory to reassure his soul that nothing is ever lost.

Christopher took his father's hand again and told him, "We will be right here waiting for you when your time comes."

As they stood there, Asher was so amazed by the extravagant beauty of his surroundings and the warmth, love and peace he felt in his tattered heart, that a tear escaped his eye and he longed to stay there forever. Just then, as he wiped at his cheek, he heard a soft voice behind him call his name. He knew that voice and his heart leapt inside him when he turned and found his dear Katherine smiling before him.

"Oh Katie," he called choked with emotion.

"My darling Asher," she said. "How dear you are to me."

She then soothed him with words of assurance that the peace and love he was feeling is eternal; a gift from a just and merciful God who holds those he loves in the palm of his hand, never to be taken from him or his presence. She spoke of his bravery and fortitude in never losing faith as all he had known and loved had been ripped from his life. And that God had walked with him through his lost days of pain and sorrow.

Asher was so filled with emotion that he could not speak. Soon, the gentleman who had greeted him in the elevator just hours before appeared at his side and told him it was time to go. His kind, gentle face shone with such love and compassion that Asher yielded to his direction as he took him by the elbow and guided him away. Katherine and Christopher waved goodbye while Asher looked longingly into their angelic faces. Once again at the door where he had first entered, the silver-haired man told Asher that God had more for him to do with his life in the immediate days ahead that would find their anchor in the souls of his past.

"Stay prayerful and God will lead you where you are to go," he said. Just as Asher was about to ask a question, the man disappeared and the door closed, leaving him alone in the dingy, darkened hallway.

For the next few days Asher was unable to pull himself out of the reverie he was feeling and to do much else but reflect on all that had happened to him. Luckily, he had accrued some leave time at work and was able to take advantage of some downtime to be by himself. He was so curious about what God may have in mind for him to do, that would in some way be tied to his past and the family he had lost.

He wrestled with his longing and need to be with his loved ones to the point that he had gone in the car one afternoon back to Wayfair Street, to see if he could make that remarkable connection again. When he arrived at the location and entered the warehouse entrance he found himself standing in a huge vacant space where the hallway and doors had been. They were simply gone, or had they ever really existed? He now felt a sensation of panic set in, was he actually losing his mind? When he arrived back home that day, he fell on his knees and begged God to help him sort it all out. While he prayed, a sense of peace and calm enveloped his soul and he came to understand that all those sevens concerning the day, time and address of his meeting was for a divine purpose, for seven is God's number of completeness and God was on his way to making him whole again. He had received the assurance he needed.

In the weeks and months that followed, Asher found himself again fully engaged with his work and career. Due to a high-stakes venture with two large medical research and development groups Asher was working with, an invitation came to sit on the board of directors for a leukemia foundation that was seeking funds for a promising cure through their bone marrow division. Asher was in a position to broker substantial funding their way that if successful, could eventually impact the lives of millions of people in the US and around the world.

Over time, Asher was able to use his amazing skills and wide range of influence in remarkable ways, and was drawn into working with other groups that had extended ramifications of this terrible disease. One such group was an orphanage that sheltered children left abandoned by parents who had suffered and died of leukemia and other lethal forms of cancer. Eventually, he adopted five-year-old Jason and seven-year-old Mandy and gave them a life full of love and encouragement.

God, in his abundant grace, had intervened into an existence smoldering in pain and loss, creating new purpose and life. In these watershed moments of revealed love by the Father, great and mighty things are possible. We are never lost to him and we are truly never alone. Through his extravagant mercies, the wounds of the heart and soul can be restored with renewed strength and vitality; for to each is given a divine destiny to fulfill. Beauty for ashes.

They say that true love transcends all time. Crawling from the deep void that had come to define him, Sonny Boone, a young man from the South, fights to regain the life he once knew. He toils against the shadowy underworld in his own mind, searching for redemption, clarity, and wholeness. He is but one soul passing through this verdant realm; known, loved, and remembered, with his unique story to tell in **Savannah**.

SAVANNAH

*I*n the twilight of dawn, patches of dense fog hover over the long stretch of coastal marshland, shrouding the sawgrass and tidal pools in an eerie, buffered silence. Water moves slowly into shallow recesses, nurturing the delinquent balance of life that is there by the relentless flow of the tide, seeping, crawling, and expanding into every crevice and byway, while holding the sea at bay. Mingled in the briny scent of salt, ghostlike water fowl hunt and peck their way through the thick mist. With vigilance, they search the water now swelling at their feet. Hidden in the far distance, a dense subtropical forest embellished with ancient oaks towers upward, their sprawling branches weeping under the burden of Spanish moss they carry. The call of a hawk slices the early morning silence and there is a flutter and shutter resonating from the tree line, a disturbance present, then gone at once. This ageless wet place resides in a tireless rhythm of ebb and flow, marked in time by its enduring presence, a gift from glory.

Nestled deep within the intimate confines of this lush, dramatic landscape of coastal Georgia sits the colonial city of Savannah, with its wrought-iron gates, sprawling cobblestone streets and charming courtyards. It has beautiful interlocking city gardens, a progression of small-town squares that is held in balance by the Savannah River at one end, and marshland and sea at the other. The air is thick and warm with the fragrant scent of jasmine and magnolias that lend themselves to the cities undeniable romance and grace, marked with the bygone era of the Antebellum South that so permeates her very foundation. Many souls have come and gone over time in this unique place; digging their hands and feet into her sandy loam, drinking in her rich sustenance and passing through this verdant, pungent realm. Each generation having their own stories to tell their legacies to pass on. Some have died with their secrets untold. But it was on just such an early blush of a morning as this, that one life began, marking its course into a future uncertain, into a world that was restrained only by words unspoken, circumstances held captive and frozen in memory, the pain of their reality denied.

It was late September 1947 when the overbearing, oppressive heat of summer began to lift and the promise of cooler fall weather was in the air. They had started in the dark seclusion of her room at 3:30 a.m, the intermittent pains that first woke her up, that by 4:30 a.m. had developed into the full drama of labor. This being Gina's first child, she hadn't really known what to expect, even though those around her who did know had tried to explain. It was far worse and more terrifying than she had ever experienced or imagined. Her mother Carol and her father Art Harris had gently led her to the back seat of Art's old Plymouth and tucked a large towel under her in case her water broke on the way to town. As they move along the curving rural road in the darkened predawn, Gina cried out, as her mother who sat beside her tried to comfort her young frightened daughter.

As they entered town that morning the fog was thick over the Savannah River. Steamy, writhing in the slight breeze from the south, it swirled up over the road on the bridge, then moved on with the stream. Anxiously Art pulled up in front of the emergency entrance to the hospital and Carol went to alert the staff inside of their arrival. Art tried to help his daughter from the car. Deep in his heart, Art wished for this birthing to be over and done with, unhappy that the burden of this moment had been placed in his hands to deal with. Where was Sonny, the father of this child about to be born? Why wasn't he here to see Gina through this tumultuous time he had helped to create?

Gina was just barely eighteen and had little life experience when she had met Sonny a little over a year ago. The war was finally over and many of the young men returning home were sad and needy; their eyes darting and anxious having seen too much of the horrors of war, their souls marked forever with the indelible images of carnage, devastation, and death. Sonny had been one of those who would need nurturing and Gina, who from childhood had always taken in stray kittens and fed feral dogs that came up in the yard, was automatically drawn to Sonny, whom she thought could surely be put back together with enough love and care. But where was he now?

At 6:05 a.m., weighing in at five pounds and two ounces, and twenty-one inches long, Sonny's baby boy squalled out his first sounds of life, much to the relief of his exhausted young mother who now cried more from the ease of her pain than joy for the arrival of her child, so wanted, yet not wanted at the same time.

Carol and Art stayed with their daughter for the first hour after the birth then departed for home as Gina settled in for a well-earned nap. On the way home, Carol could see the familiar grimace on Art's face and knew all too well what he was thinking as they headed back over the bridge and out of town. She had been told clearly enough for months now, as Gina's pregnancy progressed, how her husband felt about it. Now that the baby was a reality, she sat alone beside Art, in palpable silence. She too now quietly grieved for her daughter.

As a young girl, Gina had always loved the County Fair. It was a chance to meet with friends, eat her weight in cotton candy and ride the Ferris wheel, her personal favorite on the midway. As she stood near an arcade looking at the prizes all lit up in a cage, hoping to entice passers-by with a chance to win; Gina's best friend Susan Clayton waved as she ran up to Gina, introducing her to the two male companions with her.

Bob Sorenson had a dark complexion with wavy black hair. He was an athletic, good-looking young man who was Susan's cousin from Richmond Hill, a few miles south west of Savannah.

His friend Sonny Boone was tall and lanky with blond hair, and had a shy, nervous James Dean look. As the four conversed and got acquainted, they moved down the midway taking in the sights, laughing and deciding what to do next. After whirling around on most of the rides and taking in the agricultural exhibits, all four were famished and sought out the food stands near the beer garden. As they sat under the strung lights that now hid the starry sky from view, they munched on their food, listened to the music coming from the near-by dance hall and talked about their dreams and the future that stood before them now that the war was over.

Sonny was twenty-two, just six months older than his friend Bob whom he had met in the service while stationed in Évreux, France, right before the end of the of hostilities and the liberation of Paris. Bob had been an administrator attached to a bomber squadron for most of his deployment, but Sonny had fought with an armor division that crisscrossed over the borders of France and Germany the last eighteen months of the war.

The girls were fascinated to hear about their experiences but soon noticed the pained look on Sonny's face as he finally changed the subject by offering to buy more goodies to eat for anyone who wasn't stuffed already. They all laughed, declining, as they rubbed their tummies and stood to clear the table. Bob suggested that they go in to the dance hall and Jitter-Bug off their supper while they could still walk and so they did. The band that night was from Charleston, South Carolina, a group called the Baxley Band, and they really kept the music rolling. The four changed partners throughout the evening and had the best time moving to the beat of tunes like the "Chattanooga Choo-Choo," with their supple, energetic bodies.

After the austerity of the war years, it was great to be young and alive and have hope for a future that looked questionable just a few short months ago. When the music changed to a dreamy slow dance, Sonny asked Gina to take the floor one more time. As he took her in his arms, there was a look of tender longing on his face. They swayed to the music and he could not help putting his face into her soft, flowing curls and closing his eyes to let the moment carry him far away from where he had been, to a place that was soft, sweet and gentle, where all seemed right with the world again. Later as they all walked to the parking lot to say their goodbyes, Sonny asked to see Gina again and she happily agreed, giving him her address as she smiled, waved and pulled away into the night.

Two days later after their introduction at the Fair, Sonny Boone drove up the drive at Gina's home. He had followed her directions just fine, connecting with the rural route just outside of town and looking for the mail box with the hand plow attached to its post for added decoration, and a wooden plaque that dangled from the box announcing the number 174 with the name Harris in bold black letters; all a creation of Gina's father, who thought himself to have a creative eye.

Sonny parked his 1940 black Ford convertible in the driveway, turned off the radio and put out his cigarette. Popping some gum in his mouth, he checked in the mirror while slicking back his wind-blown

hair with the palms of his hands. As he got out of the car and began
to walk across the lawn toward the house, Carol, Gina's mother came
out onto the front porch with a watering can in her hand to water
her flowers. Looking up she saw the young man and waited for him
to approach the steps. Smiling he reached out his hand, and Carol put
down her watering can next to her bright pink geraniums and took
his hand. Sonny introduced himself and asked if Gina was at home, to
which Carol replied that she was and that he could find her around
back, in the vegetable garden.

As Sonny moved around the corner of the house, he could see Gina
crouched down pulling weeds and thinning okra plants. She looked so
adorable with a kerchief tied around her hair, dressed in what looked
like overalls that were rolled up to the knees and caked with damp soil.
As she stood, she pulled off her gloves and reached to wipe the sweat
from her forehead when she turned and saw Sonny walking across the
lawn. At first she smiled, then remembering her appearance, she quickly
grabbed the scarf from her head and began to tidy herself. This made
Sonny laugh and a smile lit his face.

Carol soon came out of the back door of the house with a tall pitcher
of iced tea and glasses on a tray, placing them on a small picnic table
under an elm tree that grew near the garden. At that point Art, Gina's
dad, came out of the garden shed with a spade he had just sharpened
and saw that they had company. Carol motioned to Art to take a break
and have some tea to cool off.

As everyone coalesced under the elm, a slight breeze brought
momentary relief from the hot Georgia noonday sun, and everyone
gladly reached for their tea. Gina happily introduced Sonny to her
parents and told them how they had met at the fair through her friend
Susan Clayton, whom her parents had known since Gina and Susan
were in the second grade together. Art being the typical father of an
only child and a daughter to boot scrutinized Sonny and asked about
his family, where he was from and what he had done in the service.

Sonny seemed a bit shy and reluctant to reveal much about himself.
However, during the course of this friendly interrogation, the family
came to know that Sonny Boone had grown up in the small town of
Jesup, Georgia, about two hours southwest of Savannah, where his
family was in the hardware business. He had one sibling, an older
sister named Katie, who was now married and living in Atlanta. His
parents had planned to send Sonny on to college, but the war broke

out and then everything changed. When asked by Art what he wanted to do now, he seemed uncertain and at a loss for words, finally saying something about looking into school again and some business opportunities up north.

Soon Sonny changed the subject by asking Gina if she would like to take a ride. After getting a nod from her mother, she said that she would love to but needed a few minutes to wash up and change her clothes. While Sonny patiently waited for Gina, he made an attempt to engage her parents in conversation about their garden, as he moved toward a row of leafy collard greens. Art stuck his newly sharpened spade in the ground and began a dissertation on the need for frequent irrigation of the sandy soil found near the coast.

As Sonny and Gina drove off down the lane that afternoon, Art turned to Carol with a quizzical look on his face, shook his head and walked back into the garden shed. Carol stood motionless near the picnic table for a moment, staring off over the nearby fields, remembering how it was when she was young within the flower of her womanhood, experiencing everything new for the first time. She thought about what a special season it is for every young girl and how the pure joy and sweetness of those moments is like the flicker of a candle, a wondrous, passionate glow, but once disturbed, it disappears and is gone forever. How soon it is that the realities of life settle in, shattering the naive expectations of youth.

Finally, Carol bringing herself back to the moment at hand, placed the pitcher of tea on her tray, gathered the glasses and disappeared inside. When was it she wondered, when she and Art had lost the magic between them and had settled for the mundane grind of life, the mechanics of living without the pleasure, passion and excitement that makes life worth living?

Sonny and Gina drove to a park near the river and pulled up under the shade of an oak tree, letting the slight breeze from the water sooth them. As they had driven there, they laughed and held light conversation, mostly talking about their meeting at the fair and the good time they had. But now as they sat looking out over the river, they seemed to each be lost in their own thoughts.

Finally, Sonny looked over at Gina and reached for her hand. She nervously held his hand, searched his face for any signs of what he might be thinking. Then staring straight ahead, he started out slowly, forming his words with care, unsure of how much he wanted to say to the young happy girl seated beside him. He told her that he now understood what a delicate thing life is and how in our normal passing we do not fully understand the miracle of our being, the essence of life.

"We take so much for granted," he said. The sadness in his voice made Gina wish she could make him feel better but she didn't know how. She acknowledged that what he said was true and that the war had made everyone a little more sensitive than they might have been, for all had suffered some kind of loss.

Sonny went on to say that when he was a little boy, he would lay in his bed at night and wonder what he would do when he was a grown-up man. All he knew as he grew older was that he did not want to be his dad. Even then he had felt like running, that there had to be so much more waiting for him out there in the world. He, like many small boys, dreamed of far-off places and grand adventures, of seeing how others live in far-off lands. Now turning in his seat, Sonny look into Gina's eyes and said he had seen far off places and that he now realized that at the heart of it, all people want the same things; to live, love, and laugh, to have families and grow old tending their grandchildren. Sonny said that over the last few years, he had gained a new respect for his father, his steadiness and quiet wisdom that in the past he had regarded as dull and boring.

A soft smile creased Gina's lips as she reached to pat the hand she was holding and admitted that often it is hard to fully understand and appreciate parents with their rules and concerns, but that most parents love their children and do the best they can for them. With his free hand, Sonny reached for Gina, placing his arm around her neck and gently pulled her to him and kissed her tenderly.

Over the next several weeks, Gina and Sonny became inseparable, except for the time Sonny was obligated to work for his father in his business while living at home, until he decided what he wanted to do with his future. Gina had graduated from high school in the spring and now worked for the public library as a file clerk and all-around gofer in training. When they were not at their respective jobs, they were together. Over the course of time, the two had opened their souls to one another, speaking of all their personal aspirations and desires. They found that they had so much in common, that there was a natural ease in their relationship like putting on your favorite pair of old slippers.

Gina had noticeably been good for Sonny, bringing him out of his shell and forcing him into a true belly laugh on occasion. As the two seemed to be best friends, Carol already knew that her daughter had fallen in love with Sonny and waited, wondering how soon it would be before Gina would come to her with this news. Even Art, over time, had come to see that Sonny though a quiet, private person, had a good heart and the right kind of values they all shared. And then there was the other side of it, the pure joy and delight that his daughter exhibited at the very mention of Sonny's name. Yes, Art also saw the signs and felt it would only be a matter of time before he and Sonny had the talk.

One rainy afternoon, Sonny pulled up in front of the Savannah Library with a sack lunch. After he held his coat over their heads, getting him and Gina back to his car, they settled in through the downpour and ate the hot dogs, pickles, and chips Sonny had brought. As they talked, laughed, and ate their lunch, Sonny looked over at Gina and smiled. Reaching for her face, he swiped at the mustard dancing at the corner of her mouth and with his finger, put that mustard in his own mouth saying, "Waste not, want not," to which she laughed and offered him more with a quick kiss.

Smiling at each other with mustard smeared on their faces, Sonny took Gina's hand and teased, that just by looking at her big yellow grin he could tell she was the girl for him. As Gina giggled and began to pull her hand away to wipe her face, Sonny stopped her and held on to her. When she looked into his eyes she could tell there had been a slight shift in his mood, he now seemed more deliberate.

He then faced her, putting both hands on her shoulders and with an intense looked, gazed straight into her eyes and said, "Mustard mouth, will you marry me?"

At this Gina threw her arms around his neck and squealed "Yes!"

The young couple decided to talk to Gina's parents together. Gina had invited Sonny over to the house for dinner one night and was prepared to serve cake and coffee after the meal when she and Sonny would tell her parents about their plans. That night as the meal progressed, everyone seemed in a good mood and conversation was easy. Sonny told the family about his decision to pursue a career opportunity in Indiana. He said he had heard from a friend of his, a guy he had met in the service said that the Studebaker plant in South Bend was now hiring, picking up their auto production again now that the war had ended. Sonny, for the first time, seemed excited and animated by the idea of helping the company produce a car line he had always admired. He spoke of the revolutionary bullet-nose design they had used in the production of the Champion, Commander, and Starlight models and what a success they had been.

Art said he knew that Studebaker had the reputation of being a quality car and that the mayor of Savannah actually drove one in a parade the city held downtown a few months ago. He went on to say it was a beautiful shiny robin's egg blue and the only one he had ever actually seen outside of magazines. Sonny said he loved that color. After a moment to help himself to more sweet potatoes, he continued talking about all that Studebaker had done for the war effort, like producing 200,000 Army trucks, most having been sent to France and the Soviet Union, and how they had perfected the engine used in the B-17 Flying Fortress. Art was happy to see a glint in Sonny's eyes and that he had finally begun to think about his future.

After supper they decided to sit in the living room to have their coffee and the wonderful coconut cream cake Gina had made from her mother's recipe. It had always been a favorite at the Harris household. Once they were settled and were sipping at their coffee, Gina began by telling her parents that a few days ago Sonny had asked her to marry him and that she had said yes, and she flashed a happy excited smile his way. Sonny took over at this point, explaining that with this new opportunity in South Bend, the factory was giving veterans a leg up in hiring and that he felt confident once hired, he could make enough money for them to live on. He said that he had already forwarded an application to them and should be hearing back any day. Gina crossed the room to pick up a calendar from the desk and pointed to a date just two weeks away.

Sonny then explained that the plan was for him to go north and get established, find an apartment, then dart back over a weekend and pick up Gina. By the time he came back for her, he would have money in his pocket and a place for her to live.

Art sat back in his chair and rubbed his chin, taking turns looking into Sonny and Gina's young expectant eyes, realizing their longing for each other and need to be together. He cautiously tested their emotions by asking if they had considered waiting until Sonny had his job and all the other preparations made, and then get married and not be forced to rush and make plans.

A flicker of disappointment showed in Gina's eyes, but Sonny jumped in and said he understood Art's concerns for his only daughter, but that he was going to take good care of her because she was his soul mate and that he and Gina both knew that. At this point, Carol broke in to say that she realized they sincerely loved one another but that two weeks was a very short time to put a wedding together. At that, Gina said a small gathering of family and a few of their closest friends would not require much notice for a simple ceremony that could be held in their own beautiful flower garden at home. Carol looked over to Art who had now clasped his hands and was looking down at the floor, studying the pattern of the throw rug beneath his feet. After a short silence, Art looked up and asked Sonny if he had discussed all of this with his parents. Sonny replied, "yes", and that his parents wanted to meet Gina, and that he hoped to take her home to Jesup on Saturday for an introduction and visit.

Carol then said with a sympathetic smile, "Why don't we talk again the first of the week and decide then what needs to be done."

At that, Art stood and stretched a bit, asking Sonny to walk outside with him for a moment. Gina shot her mother a distressed look as her mother began carrying their cups and dessert dishes into the kitchen, motioning for Gina to follow her and lend a hand. Washing the dishes, Gina looked out the window above the sink and saw her father across the yard under the elm tree with one foot up on a picnic bench, gesturing with his hands as he spoke to Sonny. Sonny stood there listening with his hands in his pockets, occasionally nodding his head with acknowledgement.

"I wonder what Dad is saying to Sonny?" Gina asked, while her mother rubbed her shoulder and told her not to worry. "I am going to marry him, Mom," she said as she folded the dish towel and again peered out the window.

"I know sweet girl, but let's make sure it's right," said Carol, pulling Gina into her arms for a hug.

Saturday was the next time Gina had a chance to be alone with Sonny and talk about their plans. Driving along Highway 84 toward Jesup, Gina sat snuggled beside Sonny, listening to him explain his family dynamics, down to his mother's nervous laugh and his father's tendency to constantly say "Well now," before weighing in on important matters.

Gina laughed as Sonny went through certain antics he had pulled in his youth that disturbed the calm and order of his parent's home, but all in all he felt he had a very typical childhood. Gina in a moment of seriousness asked Sonny what he and her father had talked about outside the night of their announcement.

Sonny gave her a sideways glance and said, "Man talk."

"What does that mean?" Gina asked.

"That means I can't tell you because I vowed to keep our discussion between me and your Dad."

"Is this how we are going to start out our lives together, by you keeping secrets from me?" she said.

Sonny smiled and told Gina there was another way she could look at it, that he was, in fact, a man of honor and would keep his word no matter to whom it was given, including her. She smiled back and said, "Case closed" and that she would chalk this one up to male bonding. Sonny then winked at her and drove into his parents' driveway.

Albert Boone, Sonny's father was tall and thin like his son, his bald head and glasses giving him a bookish look. Virginia, Sonny's mother, was short, plump, and sweet; bubbling with excitement to meet the girl that had so captivated her only son's heart. Invited into the parlor, they all sat while Virginia presided over distributing napkins and pouring tea. Gina smile as Virginia gave out a nervous laugh and asked if she would like one of the small sandwiches she now passed on a tray. For a while they made small talk, trying to find common ground. Gina spotted the beautiful piano that sat near the window the moment she had entered the room and asked Virginia if she played. She shook her head and said sadly no, but that she had given both of her children lessons and that they could both play fairly well. Gina was fascinated to learn this about Sonny and begged him to play something, anything. He smiled and rolled his eyes at his mother who smiled back with motherly pride and motioned him on with the wave of her hands to please play.

"Oh, all right, but just one," Sonny said as he sat down and adjusted himself to reach the pedals.

Soon the dreamy sound of Gershwin's "Rhapsody in Blue" filled the air. Gina was mesmerized as she watched Sonny play. Just as he was about to finish the piece, he all of the sudden broke into a few measures of a hot, jazzy Boogie-Woogie that ended with a flourish as he gallantly stood up and took a deep bow.

"Oh, for heaven's sake, Sonny!" his mother said, laughing as she shook her head at her mischievous boy.

When the topic of marriage finally came up, Albert made a similar argument to the one Gina's father had raised, about the two of them waiting to be wed until after Sonny got set up and the necessaries put into place. Sonny assured them that the timing was irrelevant, because he knew he was going to get hired and that he would need to get right back to his job after coming down to get Gina, who would need to be packed up and ready to go. After all he would not have any leave time as a new employee and he and Gina were anxious to begin their life together.

There was a casual yet determined tone in Sonny's voice that was all too familiar to the parents of this head strong young man who stood before them. Albert got up from his chair, and while reaching for a cigar in his breast pocket, walked over to the window. Looking out, he asked Sonny how soon he thought he would hear from the Studebaker Company. He reassured his dad that it could be any day now because he had mailed in the application his friend George had sent him over a week ago.

Turning away from the window, Albert looked at Gina and with the sincere concern of a father he said "Well now, Gina, do you really think you are ready for the life changing events that are about to take place; marriage and moving away from your family?"

Gina stood and moved to the waiting arms of Sonny who now held her tight. "Mr. Boone, I love Sonny with all my heart and I can't imagine my life without him now, we truly belong to each other" she said.

With that Sonny kissed her cheek and again reassured his dad that all their plans would work out just fine and not to worry; that he would make good. Virginia was now on her feet, walking toward the children with her arms open wide and her eyes brimming with emotion.

"Welcome to the family," she said to Gina as she embraced and kissed them both.

The wedding was an intimate affair that took place just two weeks after the Boones met their new daughter to be. Carol had been fortunate enough to arrange for the ceremony to be held at their small country church, the very place where Gina had been christened as a baby. Carol had always thought her daughter would be married in a church with flowers and she was determined to have this wedding as much for herself as for Gina. While Carol arranged Gina's veil in a tiny room off the small modest sanctuary, she smiled and thought how happy and beautiful her sweet daughter looked, soon to step over the threshold of youth and into adult life. She hoped her future would be all that Gina wished for and that the love she felt now would sustain her in difficult times that would surely come. Soon there was a rap on the door and the signal was given that all was ready to start the ceremony. As Gina emerged from her cocoon in the ante room and took her dad's arm, she literally radiated the peace and joy she felt. She was a stunning young bride and Sonny's heart skipped a beat as he saw her move down the aisle toward him.

At the reception that was later held in a hall beside the church, friends and family gathered to wish the happy couple congratulations. There was a champagne toast given by one of Sonny's friends, a confirmed bachelor who admitted that he would give the whole marriage thing another look, if he could find someone as beautiful and special as Gina. Then there was dancing, that included the in-laws taking to the floor with their son and daughter, a welcoming gesture to strengthen new familial ties. The food and flowers had in part been a contribution from the church ladies that had watched Gina grow up over the years and felt a sense of pride and joy at being part of her special day. Before the reception ended, Albert approached the young couple and while shaking Sonny's hand, passed to him an envelope with money inside and told him to use it on their short two-day honeymoon to have a very special time. Sonny grinned and reached to hug his dad while thanking him for the gift and for supporting him in this move to a new life.

After all the festivities ended, a shower of rice rained down on the happy couple as they made their get-away in Sonny's Ford that had been decorated with streamers and a "Just Married" sign. That night as the newlyweds drove off to Tybee Island and into the sea breeze, under a full moon, where Sonny had arranged for a beachfront bungalow; the two smiled at each other and Sonny said to Gina, "Now that you are truly mine, I am going to love you and keep you forever." Gina then reached over and gave Sonny a quick kiss on the cheek and told him this was the happiest day of her life. For the next two days, the couple bonded in ways they had never experienced before and their joy was complete. They walked along the beach arm-in-arm. They frolicked in the surf and made sculptures in the sand. They lay in the sun and told each other stories from their lives; and at night they danced and dined out under the stars, feeding one another, toasting their new life and future together; later making sweet tender love as a pledge of their fidelity.

Sonny's employment papers had appeared just as he thought they would, and as he finished packing for his trip, he reviewed the directives he had received concerning his starting date and where to report his first day. He had a new confidence about him and felt that the fortunes of time and circumstance were converging to support his new ambitions. Life was good and when he looked over at Gina, who was folding his shirts to fit neatly in his suitcase, he could hardly believe what was happening to him. God had truly blessed him in ways he would have never thought possible.

Walking out to his car to place his gear in the trunk, Sonny smiled at his precious young wife and a slight pang of loneliness already stirred his heart. He wished he could scoop her up and take her with him right now, but that wouldn't be right. He had to press on, to make a way for her, keeping in mind her security, comfort, and personal needs.

When they embraced for the last time, it was of course bittersweet and slightly tearful on Gina's part, who tried to keep up a brave front, so Sonny could bear their parting and know she would be all right for the few short weeks he would be away. While Sonny pulled out of the driveway of his parents' home that morning, where he and Gina had stayed for the few days after their honeymoon; he waved and smiled to see that his parents had already closed ranks around Gina, holding her in their arms. They all three waved back at him, then he was gone.

Sonny had planned to give himself four days to reach his destination, heading northwest to Columbia, South Carolina; then on to Asheville, North Carolina; Lexington, Kentucky; Fort Wayne, Indiana; then on into South Bend. As he drove along, he replayed in his mind the events of the last few months since Gina had come into his life, a special time that had been such a grounding experience for him; giving him a firm foundation from which to build a new life and career. When he thought about working for the Studebaker Company, he grinned and marveled at how this German immigrant family over the centuries had lived out the American dream.

A group of brothers had started by heading for the new land of opportunity in the Americas during the late 1700s. They first worked at farming and then became blacksmiths. Later on, by developing their skills, they started a wagon-building business, and by the time the horseless carriage was established as the wave of the future, they took the next step and moved into automobile manufacturing. Yes, theirs was an impressive personal story of triumph and innovation and he couldn't wait to be a part of it. So as Sonny moved along down the stretch of highway before him, he was filled with optimism and a profound sense of gratitude.

As the first week and then a second came then went without hearing a word from Sonny, Gina, her parents and the Boone family began to wonder if everything was all right and if Sonny had indeed arrived in South Bend as planned to started his job. At the frantic bidding of Gina, Mr. Boone placed a long-distance call to the Studebaker Company and made an inquiry. To his utter shock and amazement, he learned that Sonny had never reported to the job and that they too were wondering why they hadn't heard from him and as a result had eventually filled the position held for him with another applicant. At this news, utter panic set in on all fronts.

A missing person's report was filed with local police and the state authorities were alerted as well. Gina, who had returned to her parents' home to prepare for her own departure, now sat with an open trunk and a pile of suitcases stacked in the corner of her room staring back at her, as a glaring reality that she may not be going anywhere. Through her tear-filled eyes she walked from room to room for several days, unable to concentrate, ringing her hands, stopping only momentarily to check out the window for Sonny's car. She tossed and turned at night and could not sleep, and when she did nod off through pure exhaustion, she woke up startled calling Sonny's name.

Carol tried to get Gina to sit and have a meal, but she often refused, and when she did finally settle, she merely pushed the food around on her plate. Gina's parents were becoming as much concerned for the well-being of their daughter as they were for Sonny. Gina was making herself sick with grief and refused to be comforted. Art was especially at a loss. Being more of a pragmatic man, he wanted to jump in and fix this and move on, but there was no fixing this unimaginable state of affairs. His daughter was falling apart before his eyes, his son-in-law had disappeared and he found himself at a total loss for words and no way to make things right. His heart bled for the young couple who had the world by the tail just a few short days ago. Carol was also in shock and ineffectual in helping her daughter cope which added to her overall sense of despair and helplessness.

A month after Sonny's disappearance, Carol went through the house looking for Gina one morning and could not find her. Glancing out her bedroom windows that overlooked the backyard, she saw her going into the garden shed. Carol followed Gina and when she caught up with her, found her huddled in an old wicker chair by the door weeping deep uncontrollable sobs. Kneeling down in front of Gina, Carol lifted her chin, and looked into her eyes asking in a gentle voice, what had caused this new round of tears. Gina looked at her mother and strained for words that would not come. Carol put her arms around her daughter and held her until all of her tears had been spilled.

Finally regaining enough composure to speak, Gina looked at her mother and said, "I think I am pregnant."

The months came and went with no word from Sonny or the authorities, who had ultimately moved his missing person's report into the dead case file. Gina lost all of her desire to interact with others and spent her days held up in her room, reading and sleeping or gazing out the window looking for the one who never appeared. As her belly grew, so did her despair. One afternoon when her father came in from working in his hay field, he asked Carol about Gina and what she had been doing all day, which caused a heated argument between them.

Art was growing impatient with his moping, depressed daughter and thought she should have pulled herself together by now, finally realizing Sonny was now gone from her life and that she should return to her job at the library. And he was none too happy about her pregnancy either, reminding her often that he had advised her that she and Sonny should have waited to marry, until after he got established. If she had only done as he had counseled, she would not have the added burden of a child on the way that she alone would now be responsible for.

Carol argued back that Art should try to have more compassion for Gina, realizing all she was going through would be hard for anyone but especially a young girl her age. At that, Art replied that she had better get a grip pretty soon because like it or not, it wasn't just about Gina anymore and with that, he turned and walked out of the kitchen, slamming the door behind him. Gina had overheard many of these episodes between her parents in recent days that now added guilt to her misery.

As the lazy sun yawned and stretched its rays through the hospital window early one morning, the nurse brought Gina her baby boy and encouraged her once again to try nursing the little guy who still had no name on his birth certificate. Each time she had been asked what they should put on paper, she seemed uninspired and detached from the realities of motherhood with all of its consequences and responsibilities, and instead chose to drift off to someplace of her own making, where she didn't have to think at all. When Art and Carol came into visit on the third day of Gina's hospitalization, the doctor took them aside and told them that it appeared Gina was suffering from postpartum depression, and was not interacting with her newborn in the expected way, making the nurturing and bonding process more difficult for the infant.

Art, with a look of exasperation on his face, raked his hands through his hair and asked what could be done to help Gina get back on her feet. The doctor went on to explain that this problem occurs from time to time in a small percentage of women and that love, support and time were about the only things he could recommend. At this Art began to pace up and down in short strolls staring at the floor. Finally, Carol reached out and put her hand on his arm to stop him.

With a searching, pleading look in her eyes she quietly said to him, "We can do this."

With a resigned sigh he looked back at her and said, "I guess we will have to!"

When Gina returned home, her room had been refreshed with bright new curtains at her windows and a new spread for her bed, evidence of the fresh start the Harris's hoped to make. On Gina's dresser was an arrangement of fragrant fresh-cut flowers with a card from the Boones wishing her well and asking for a visit. Over in the corner was a bassinette Carol's church friends had provided and furnished with crisp linens and soft baby blankets all in blue. Over the bed hung a painted plaque decorated with cherubs that said, "Welcome Home Samuel," the name the family had collectively settled on.

As Gina entered the room holding the baby, a look of surprise washed her face and a hint of a smile brushed her lips as she placed Samuel in his new bed. She also noticed her mother had taken the old wicker rocker from the garden shed and painted it a fresh white, tied a new soft cushion in its seat and placed it near Samuel's bed so that Gina could rock the baby and feed him from the bottles they had purchased when Gina gave up on nursing.

Gina walked through the room touching everything, then turned to her parents and said, "Thank you so much for doing all of this for me and Sam. It's beautiful."

Gina, in time, was able to put her life back together slowly, ever so slowly, piece by piece. Once she was home again in familiar surroundings, with her mother there to help her those first few weeks, her strength began to return and she started exhibiting new interest in her baby. Fortunately, Sam was a happy camper and only got cranky when hungry or wet. After a couple of months, he began to fill out with the usual baby fat ripples and was even known to put on a silly grin now and then that everyone seemed to enjoy. Art had swallowed his pride and came to understand that if he wanted any degree of normalcy restored to his home, that he had to be part of the process, and so had consented to hold Sam while a bottle was prepared or keep an eye on him as he slept in his tiny bed while Gina washed diapers and hung them out on the line in the yard, a daily operation. Over the course of the ensuing days and months, a new rhythm of living took hold at the Harris home, and they all slowly emerged from their gut-wrenching ordeal of loss, and began inching forward toward the promise of a new day, a better way.

Carol sat out under the elm tree late one afternoon feeding Sam some crackers and peanut butter that he had summarily smeared all over on his happy little round face. Gina came out the back door of the house having just returned home from her work at the library, where over the last two years, she had honed her skills and been made an assistant librarian. Sam, a toddler now, looked up to see his mother's approach and let out a joyful squeal as he ran toward her with his short little legs and outstretched arms. As Gina bent down and scooped him up into her arms, she kissed his peanut butter face and told him what a tasty little muffin he was, as he laughed and hugged her neck.

Art had been in the garden picking vegetables for dinner when he heard Sam yell "Papa!" and looked up to see Sam coming across the lawn with a cracker in his hand. Placing the vegetables in a basket, he sat down on the edge of the grass where Sam found him sprawled out to rest. As Sam came up to Art, he held out his crispy offering and Art obediently opened his mouth as Sam stuck the cracker inside with a happy grin and giggle. Art chewed on the cracker saying "Yum yum," then grabbed Sam and wrestled around with him on the lawn as Sam laughed with glee. How could any of them have ever thought this little man to be anything but the blessing and miracle he was? Art, who had started out in a hard place, had come full circle and now enjoyed Sam as the son he never had. He had completely bonded with this child and loved it when Sam toddled along behind him wanting to see what Papa was doing and could he help. Because of Sam's pure sweetness, Carol and Art had found a common bond of joy in him that enhanced their own personal relationship and the pleasure they found in him seemed to translate into many other areas of their lives.

But what had happened to Sonny Boone? As the last two-and-a-half years had slowly slipped away into the shadowy recesses of memory, they were no longer defined by a constant agony of the soul. Gina would still lay awake in her bed at night and wonder what had happened to her dear Sonny, whom she had loved nearly more than life itself. Every time she looked into Sam's sweet, tender face she saw Sonny smiling back at her. At least he had left her some small treasure of himself, a testament to his passage through this mortal life that had touched her own like a shooting star, here then gone. Gina had matured quickly through the exquisite pain of her loss, and now all that really mattered was Sam. However, with every beat of her heart the question lingered, what happened to Sonny? She knew she would never be free of that question, now hidden in her secret place of her passion lost in time.

Pushing on down the thin band of road that was Highway 176, leading to the foothills outside of Ashville, North Carolina, Sonny drove with his elbow propped on the open window of his car door while smoking his last cigarette. He had pledged to Gina, that when his last pack was gone, he would buy no more. He had the radio on and the mellow tones of the Glenn Miller band playing "Moonlight Serenade" filled the car and again his thoughts were of his darling bride he had reluctantly left behind. He really wanted to be the man Gina thought he was. He wanted to make good and give her the moon on a silver platter, though that is never what she would have asked for. No, he alone had been the glowing orb in her life and he felt so proud and happy that she had chosen to spend the rest of her life with him.

A fiery dusk lit the tops of the hills now, washing the land in deep purple shadows as Sonny steered his car off the road at a Hendersonville truck stop at the edge of town. He hadn't bothered to eat since early morning and so with his grits and eggs long gone, he decided it was time to take a break and have a bite to eat. There were several cars and trucks parked outside the café; with a few long-haul semis in a side parking lot. As he walked in and took a seat at a booth near the back wall, a middle-aged woman in a pink and green uniform approached his table placing a glass of water and utensils in front of him and smiling asked if he would like to see a menu. Sonny listened to the offered specials and settled for an open-faced beef sandwich and a cup of coffee. When the waitress returned with Sonny's order she made small talk with him and asked if he was from around here, Sonny mentioned he was traveling and just passing through.

As he ate his supper, he casually looked around the busy café and noticed what a diverse group of people had flocked to its neon sign this particular night. Up at the front near the windows sat a young rambunctious family with squirmy little ones that kept wiggling out of their seats, and while their mother made a feeble attempt to round them up and put them back in their chairs, her husband seemed oblivious as to what was going on around him.

Along the right wall, two little old ladies sipped at coffee and ate cherry pie as they swapped stories about their grandkids, one pointing to a picture she had pulled from her purse. To the left, two large burly men seemed to be in an animated dispute, one gesturing wildly in the air, saying something about a fish. There was a young couple at the counter having a first date, laughing and talking over a large pile of French fries and Cokes. As Sonny stood to stretch and go pay his bill, he put some tip money down on the table and began to walk toward the front check-out counter. As he walked he noticed his waitress engaged in a conversation with a man and they were both staring straight at him. When Sonny pulled out his wallet and withdrew a few dollars to cover his meal, the man stood nearby and continued to look at Sonny.

With his business completed, Sonny walked out the door and as he stood outside in the glare of the neon lights, he stretched again and wondered if he should go ahead and call it a night and check into one of the tourist cabins he had passed just a mile down on the right. While Sonny crossed the parking lot to reach his car, he thought how nice it would feel to lay down now and start out again in the morning, and he fished for his keys from his pocket.

Then he was down, his face pushed into the gravel, his head bleeding from a severe blow to the back of his head. Shooting pains racked his body as he was repeatedly kicked while his keys and wallet were taken from him. Soon everything was swirling around him. Nausea in his stomach now rose to his throat, threatening to choke him. With a final boot to his cracked skull he was out and gone, swallowed by a deep void where all perception had vanished. The two men that beat Sonny and left him for dead in the dark parking lot that night, sped away in his car over a small country Carolina road and disappeared into the dark.

It was over an hour that Sonny lay in a heap, unconscious and bleeding, unable to move before he was discovered by a guest from the café. A lady, who had initially been parked next to Sonny's car, now spotted him lying on the ground where his car had been. Seeing Sonny's serious condition, the gray-haired grandma scurried back inside the café and asked for help as she grabbed a phone that hung on the wall. By the time the police and ambulance had arrived, several people from inside the café were huddled around Sonny, some trying as best they could to offer comfort and encouragement while others stared in total shock and horror at the poor man on the ground. Many could not believe that something like this could happen in their small-town neighborhood. Once the word got out, would anyone feel safe here at night again?

With a screaming siren and flashing lights, the ambulance rushed up to the emergency door at Asheville Memorial and quickly off loaded their patient. With a swift alert from the emergency room, Dr. Walters, who was on duty that night, barked orders at his staff to start an IV, draw bloodwork and order X-rays stat. Walters, a veteran of the trauma unit, had seen it all, but this was bad.

"Who would do this to another human being?" he asked, as he and his nurse removed Sonny's clothing to make an appraisal of his multiple contusions and possible broken bones. Sonny's vitals were weak and erratic at best, further complicating his delicate condition.

For the next several hours, the OR medical team struggled to put Sonny back together; supplying three pints of blood to his battered system as they worked to mend damaged organs and bone fractures. On top of all the bodily damage he had suffered, he also had a bad concussion and skull fracture that put him into a deep state of unconsciousness. Four hours later, walking out of the OR, Dr. Walters could only hope that Sonny's youth and an otherwise healthy body would be on his side and help to pull him through. For the next twelve days Sonny laid in his hospital bed unaware of the world around him as night changed to day, then back into night, he floated on the edge of reality in a no-man's land he did not recognize or comprehend, a state of being and not.

In late afternoon of the twelfth day of his ordeal, Sonny's eyes opened to see a strange young woman leaning over him adjusting a tube that seemed to be attached to his arm. He tried to speak but his mouth was so dry he could not adequately form his words, and only a groan escaped his lips which caught the nurse by surprise. More moans came from Sonny, as nurse Ellen Ames reached to give him a sip of water. Ellen smiled and tried to reassure Sonny that he was safe and all right and that he was being well cared for, when she noticed the troubled look of panic settling on Sonny's face. She took his hand and gently explained that he had been involved in a mugging and robbery a few days ago and had undergone surgery to mend his wounds.

She immediately contacted Dr. Walters about Sonny's alert condition and soon he too stood near Sonny's bedside and told him he had been unconscious due to head trauma and that his injuries and head issues would hopefully resolve themselves over time. However, the next few days revealed the fact that Sonny no longer knew who he was or where he had come from or what had happened to him. He was a ship without a rudder, set adrift on a sea of uncertainty, into an empty void that now defined his life.

When Sonny Boone was finally discharged from the hospital, he was given a note by Dr. Walters with the address of a Catholic Church mission written on it, where he could find food, shelter and counseling. Father Edward Rodgers' name had been scratched on the paper as a contact person for Sonny to see on arrival. Ed, as he liked to be called, was circling a pile of dirty dish in the mission kitchen after the noon meal when Sonny found him, having been directed there by an altar boy tending to his chores in the sanctuary.

Ed looked up and saw Sonny standing in the kitchen doorway with his hat in his hands, curling its brim nervously with his fingers. With two giant strides to match his large bulky physique, Ed crossed the floor and with a warm and understanding smile extended his hand and introduced himself. Escorted into Father Ed's study just off the small chapel behind the main church facility, Sonny was motioned to a seat near Ed's desk and offered a cup of coffee from a console table near a window that overlooked an expansive lawn and hedged garden. Sonny gratefully took the cup and sipped in its deep, rich comfort. Ed took up his own cup and studied Sonny as he sat down in his chair. Ed explained that he had conversed with Dr. Walters and had been filled in on the details of Sonny's circumstance.

As he looked over the brim of his cup, he asked Sonny how he was feeling about things and what he might like to do. Sonny confided that he really didn't know where to start to put his life back together, having no clue as to who he was or where he belonged. And then there was the associated fear of discovery, and that he might not like what he might find out at some point. Ed assured Sonny that he could stay at the mission as long as he had a need and that there was always a demand for helping hands to earn his keep. Sonny soon relaxed and appreciated the warm, easy-going manner of his host who seemed to have a true desire to be of help.

In the weeks that followed, Father Ed had given Sonny the nickname Thomas, after a faithful man in the Bible, a disciple of Jesus who had also struggled with doubts of uncertainty yet in the end had prevailed. Sonny had been appointed a job working as a groundskeeper, under the guidance of an older gentleman by the name of Rich Ricker, a widower, who had retired a few years back and now kept the church grounds full-time. Sonny worked alongside Rich every day except Saturdays and Sundays that were set aside for rest and worship. Sonny lived out of a barracks hall set up behind the rectory for people in need who were passing through.

Usually in the late afternoons, Father Ed would call Sonny to his study, where they would have coffee together and talk about Sonny's situation. Often, the two would pray asking God for a blessing of restoration. Ed had contacted a parishioner who was a neurologist and asked him to meet with Sonny. Dr. Jim Jefferson discuss triggers that might help refresh his memory, and described how certain sounds, smells, and objects can stir sensory perceptions that can often lead to memories. Sonny was encouraged to keep a journal and jot down any flashback or thoughts he might have and their sources. By this time, weeks had turned into months and still Sonny languished in the darkened regions of his mind, which held his true identity captive and secret. When alone, he passionately implored God for his mercy, to restore his shattered memory and continue to heal his battered body. The information he had been given at the hospital was sketchy. He had been told the attack took place at a truck stop out of town but no one seemed to know where that was. For some reason, he had never talked to the police, so he was left without a clue as to where he had actually been during the robbery or where he had traveled from. How had the investigation of his case fallen through the crack? Although it was now 1949, Sonny had no frame of reference with which to look back or forward, his life remained a mystery. He was consigned to move in the shadows of a vibrant life once lived.

One Saturday night, Sonny and Rich decided to go see a movie at the local cinema. A war film was playing about D-Day and the Normandy invasion. Rich mentioned, as he reached for some popcorn, that he had been too old to enlist when the war started but that he really admired those who had gone and served. As the film got going into its first full battle sequence, Sonny began to feel agitated, then very nervous as the scene escalated with bombs pounding the ground and aircraft circling in the air, with men yelling as they rushed the beach. At this point Sonny panicked and yelled out in an astonishing cry as he leapt from his seat and rushed out of the theater. Rich jumped up in hot pursuit of Sonny and soon found him sitting on the sidewalk, crumpled against the front wall of the theater, curled into a ball; his arms and hands flung over his head as he frantically called out "Get down, they're on your left, get down, get down."

Passersby stared at the two men as Rich put his arms around Sonny and reassured him everything was all right. After several minutes Sonny finally regained some composure, as he held on to Rich's arm and began to realize where he was and eventually struggled to his feet with Rich's help. Sonny stood trembling, shaking his head and looking at the ground as if to find the answers for what just happened in the pavers at his feet, but they yielded no answers. Rich finally got Sonny back to his car and drove him to the church barracks and saw him comfortably inside and settled, then went in search of Father Ed, whose study light glowed across the darkened court yard.

After describing to Ed the events at the theater that night, they both returned to the barracks building to check on Sonny. The two men knocked at the corner of his enclosure and asked if they could come in. Sonny said, "Yes." They found him in his darkened room stretched out on the bed, his arms folded over his eyes and resting. Ed pulled up a side chair and began to gently ask Sonny about what had happened that night and what he was feeling. Sonny said that after the film began, he started to have flashbacks and saw himself in the heat of combat with mortars going off all around him. His armor division was bivouacked at the edge of a forested area outside the city of Cologne, Germany, where there had been earlier skirmishes involving the infantry. There were trenches dug and barbed wire strung around a small perimeter of bunkers. Suddenly there was a barrage of gun fire, then heavy bombardment.

"As I scrambled to get back into my tank," he said, "There were terrible deafening explosions going on all around me, then I heard the voice of another soldier wild with fear call out to me, 'Sonny, help me

I'm stuck, please help me,' as he tugged on a section of barbed wire that had caught his left leg and ensnared his boot."

Sonny sat up on the edge of the bed trembling, with tears in his eyes and said, "I tried to make my way back to help, when there was another terrible explosion and then, he was gone."

Wiping at the tears on his pain-filled, dejected face he said, "My name is Sonny Boone. I was in the Army during the war."

Ed and Rich looked at one another in amazement and Ed asked in a calm quiet voice if there was any more about himself he could remember now, but he shook his head and said, "Sadly no."

Two years had come and gone since Sonny had been assaulted and little more progress had been made into his identity. But now with this recent revelation of his name and the fact he must have served in the Army, he had a place to start an inquiry. He wrote a letter to the Department of the Army in Washington, D.C. explaining his problem and requesting any information they might have on him. When there was no immediate response, Sonny became impatient. Then one day, he decided it was time to move on and try to build a life for himself outside the shelter of his mission home and Father Ed, who had become his closest friend and confidant. And although it would be hard to leave behind the people who had become his lifeline during his darkest hours of need, he felt compelled to make something of the miracle of life he had been so graciously given again after such a terrible, brutal attack. He wanted his life to count for something, he just didn't know what, but he knew in his heart he had to go look for it.

During his spare time in the last few weeks, Sonny had been pouring over the newspaper want ads to find work and ran on to a job offer by a freight line promising top wages along with two weeks big rig training. Moving with the urge inside himself to travel and explore, he decided to make a few phone calls and was soon off to an interview. Three days later, after being hired, he waved goodbye to Ed and the staff at the mission, as Rich drove him to the depot for his driver's training. For the next six months, Sonny traveled the highways and byways of the Midwest, delivering a variety of products to businesses and industries in small and large town across the farm belt. From the rolling verdant hills of the Mideast to the golden flat lands of grain in the Midwest, he moved along, always attempting to fill the emptiness at his core, aching questions inside him that still went unanswered; where had he come from, did he have a family, where did he belong? The relentless miles came and went as one season changed into another and yet the longing remained.

Early one morning, Sonny pulled his rig into a truck stop in Topeka, Kansas, to refuel and check in with the home office concerning his next assignment. The dispatcher explained that one of the men on the southern run was taking a week off to be home with his wife who was about to deliver their first child, and someone would need to take care of his orders for a few days. Sonny was told deliver his load in Kansas City then head southeast to Ashville, North Carolina, then Charleston, South Carolina, and on to Savannah Georgia. The dispatcher concluded that there might be a need to then head for Jacksonville, Florida, where there was potential cargo at Mayport, but he would let him know.

As Sonny plotted his course through Missouri and Tennessee to deliver his first supplies in Ashville, he reminisced about the mission and his friend Father Ed in Ashville but decided not to contact him as his schedule would be tight. He had made a point to send Ed a postcard now and then wherever he might be on the road, just to say hello and let him know he was okay, a way to stay in touch. He vowed to do that again from the southland. Sonny would never forget all Ed had done for him and hoped that in the future sometime, under much brighter circumstances; they could have a real reunion.

After making the first drop of his journey, Sonny traveled on down Highway 176 just south of Ashville and decided to have dinner at a truck stop café with a large glowing neon sign, where he saw other semis parked in a side lot. When he pulled in along the other big rigs and killed his engine, he rubbed his face with his hands and glanced in his mirror while he combed his hair. As he sat there for a moment, he checked his map and saw that he was just outside the small town of Hendersonville, then putting the map aside with some other paper work, he got out of the truck and made for the door of the café. When he stood within a few feet of the door, he got an odd feeling that he had been there before, but his travels had never taken him south, so he shrugged it off and entered the café.

Once inside, he began to have a tingling sensation and a stronger sense of recollection. He seemed to perceive where everything was located; the fountain area with its tall stools, the check-out counter and the window seats in the front of the café. Startled, with the sense of panic growing within him, he tried to calm himself and looked to find a seat. The only one available was along the back wall. When he slid into the booth, he tried to get a grip on the strange feelings that were beginning to overwhelming him. Suddenly he remembered the incident at the Ashville cinema a couple of years back that had started this same way.

As the waitress arrived at his table wearing her crisp pink and green uniform, Sonny gasped for air and thought he was going to pass out. The waitress quickly put down the water and utensils she was carrying and reached for Sonny's arm and ask if he was all right, for the color had completely left his face and he was now shaking all over. He grabbed the edge of the table and continued to gasp for air as the waitress ran to get her boss. When she rounded the corner of the kitchen door she yelled, "Dan come quick, I think one of our customers is having a seizure." Dan quickly threw down his towel and followed her to the dining room.

"Hey buddy, are you okay?" asked Dan, as he slid into the booth next to Sonny and asked if he needed a drink of water, which Sonny motioned for and drank.

Slowly, Sonny was helped to his feet and escorted into a small office off the kitchen and assisted to a cushioned chair beside the desk. Looking up at the concerned expressions on the faces of Dan and his waitress, he did his best to explain what he was feeling, memories that were so clear and vivid that they were frightening, because he was a man without a past. As Dan studied Sonny's face, now crumpled with emotion he examined the contours of his features, the slight scar below his right ear that straggled onto his jaw line.

"How did you get that scar on the jaw?" asked Dan.

After a minute or so, Sonny and Dan looked at each other and in a moment of stunning clarity, they both spoke at the same time. Sonny saying, he had been kicked in the head and Dan saying he was the man found in his parking lot a couple of years ago that had been beat up and robbed.

"Oh, my word," said the waitress, I remember that. We didn't think you were going to make it."

Sonny was shaking again as he remembered being attacked and then waking up in the Ashville Hospital.

"Oh, my word," the waitress said again "You are that poor man."

With the dinner rush nearly over, Dan fixed a plate and brought it back into his office and sat with Sonny as he tried to eat. Dan filled him in on the details of that tragic night he was attacked, as best he could remember. He said he was nearly beaten to death right outside his door and how terrible he felt about that. He mentioned that while Sonny was still in the hospital, he had traveled to Ashville to see him but that he was still unconscious and they had no idea if he would ever wake up. Sonny wiped his mouth, leaned back in the chair and stared at Dan.

He thanked him for his understanding and told him how hard it was to live with huge chunks of his life missing, to which Dan said, "I can't even imagine, you are just so lucky to be alive. Two others were not as fortunate as you."

"What do you mean two others?" asked Sonny. "About the same time as your robbery, there was a string of others, a man and his son were attacked and killed one night coming out of a grocery store," said Dan. "Finally, that ring of thugs was apprehended and tried. Thank God they are now in the State Pen where they belong," explained Dan.

Sonny commented that he thought it was odd that the police never contacted him after his mugging. Dan then said that he knew the officer who had responded to the call at the café that night, a man by the name of Fred Ellis. He went on to say that Officer Ellis had made several calls up to the Ashville Hospital asking about Sonny and his condition, for he was anxious to interview him on the chance he had seen or heard something that would help in his investigation, but every time he inquired he was told, the patient was still unconscious.

In the meantime there continued to be more incidents of the same kind and the small, two-man, Hendersonville police station, was forced to move on with the hot cases they were dealing with, Ashville not being in their jurisdiction.

Dan said, "It was later concluded, because of the similarities in all these cases, including yours, Sonny, that the same group had committed these crimes and once the perpetrators were caught and convicted, these cases were put to bed."

He went on to say that no one knew Sonny had suffered amnesia. It was assumed if he ever woke up, he would simply go on with his life. Dan who sat with his legs spread and his elbows resting on his knees, now webbed his hands together and stared down at the floor shaking his head and said, "I truly regret this whole sorry mess and the pain it has caused you, if you can think of any way I can help, just ask."

Early the next morning, Sonny waved goodbye to Dan as he pulled out of the café drive. The two men had sat up all night talking after locking up the diner. They then walked the short distance down the lane to Dan's home, where both men crashed for a few hours. The next morning Dan insisted on feeding Sonny a hearty breakfast and plenty of hot coffee before he hit the road, and now stood at the café door with a towel over his shoulder and his hand in the air, while Sonny pulled away over the hill and out of sight.

As he drove along that morning, Sonny reflected on his situation and took an accounting. He now knew a few important facts about himself that may eventually lead to other clues. He knew his name and that he had been in the Army during the war and now had discovered where he had nearly lost his life and why he had never talked to the police about his mugging. Bits and pieces of a puzzle that now represented his life, were slowly coming together. His continual prayer in recent weeks had been that he would hear from the Army and that the remaining pieces might reveal information that would lead him back to the life he had once known.

By the time Sonny rolled into Charleston, South Carolina, it was late in the afternoon. He had just enough time to drive to Market Street and drop his supplies before the work day ended. After his delivery, he pulled his rig into a side alley and parked it out of the way so he could take a stroll and search for some dinner. Now that he had a few minutes to himself and could think and take in the sights, he realized that he felt so comfortable here in this city that had a familiar feel. Even the smells that permeated the air, drifting down the street from the various eateries, seem so right and natural to him and it was at this point, it popped into his mind that he loved She Crab Soup. Wondering where that thought came from, he almost laughed out loud. After his supper at a sidewalk bistro, he took a short walk to a nearby park and sat on a bench to let his supper settle. Looking off across the street at the old historic buildings and beyond to the waterfront; the scent of salt on the sea breeze further aroused his senses and it slowly came to him he had been here many times before. Emotions of contentment mixed with amazement filled his soul. Later as darkness fell, he moved down US 17 toward Savannah, Georgia. On each side of this ribbon of road were large tracks of land, majestic in their isolated beauty. The dense, lush coastal marshland, only disturbed by the tide and dusk that now blackened the tree line on the horizon, was set against the flaming sky, and sea birds made for their roosts in the tall oaks and bushy palmettos. Moving along the highway Sonny put down his window and stretched his arm out into the night air while emotion brimmed in his eyes; for here in the southland, he sensed he was home.

Dense mist rose from the Savannah River the next morning as Sonny crossed its bridge looking for the marker announcing entry into the state of Georgia. Drawing closer to the city he began to feel pangs of remembering, ghostly images passing through his mind, hushed yet visible harbingers of memory still elusive, undefined yet ever present. Slowly pulling his truck over the cobblestone streets along the water front, he backed his rig up to the loading dock of a warehouse and cut his engine. As he quietly gazed across the river in the stillness of the early morning, he was flooded with feelings he could not explain or rationalize. Intuition told Sonny he needed to spend some time here, to sort things out in his mind, to uncover the longing that had now pierced his heart.

While Sonny waited for the warehouseman to arrive and open the doors, he contacted dispatch and asked about the cargo at Mayport and was told that a trucker making the Mobile-Pensacola-Jacksonville run had been able to load that shipment yesterday, so Sonny was cleared from that order. Sonny told the dispatcher he really needed to take a few days off to handle some personal business and would like to call in next week for an assignment. Reviewing the order mandates with the route supervisor, the dispatcher came back in moments confirming Sonny's leave. Brock Harmon, manager of the warehouse soon greeted Sonny with a handshake and introduction. Soon the two men headed inside to do their paper work and have some coffee.

As the semi-trailer was unloaded by warehouse workers, Brock and Sonny had a chance it visit and make small talk for a few minutes. Sonny explained that Cid Andrews the usual driver for this run was busy becoming a father, so Sonny had taken his place. Brock laughed and said he had been blessed a couple of times himself and asked if Sonny had children, to which he replied no. Then Brock looked at Sonny and said, "You know you sure look familiar for some reason. I graduated high school with a Sonny Boone over in Jesup, class of 42." "As I recall," Brock went on, "He had a good-looking older sister named Katie all the guys tried to date, and their mom and dad owned a hardware store on Main Street."

Sonny smiled and nodded, and gave no response.

Climbing back into his truck, Sonny could barely breathe. Placing both hands on the steering wheel, he rested his forehead on his hands and tried to absorb what had just happened. He had been handed some astounding information. If he was in fact the same Sonny Boone that Brock spoke of, he may indeed have a family and a home. He arranged with Brock to leave his trailer in his warehouse lot for a few days and decided he must drive to Jesup and visit this Boone Hardware store on Main Street. Coming in on Highway 84 he entered the small rural town and had no trouble locating the store. Sonny sat in the truck looking at the store front for several minutes and again began to experience those feelings of remembrance; of things familiar yet ill-defined.

Taking a deep breath, he prepared himself to enter the store, praying fate would be kind. Opening the door, he stepped over the threshold to a jingling bell, alerting those inside of a new client in from the street. Four or five people browsed the aisles, picking through bins for this and that. Near the front window, a tall gentleman with a bald head and glasses was in deep conversation with another man concerning a spring needed for his sprinkler head, an ancient rain bird that had given up the ghost. Sonny quietly walked the aisles and ended up near the back of the store where a small office was located. Through the open door he noticed a short, plump woman going over the books, her adding machine plunking away as a long tape headed over the edge of the desk toward the floor. She had a pencil tucked behind one ear, along with several strands of curly gray hair that framed her intense round face.

Suddenly, behind Sonny's back came a voice that said, "Hi, may I help you?"

Sonny quickly turned to follow the voice, as the woman in the office looked up to see who was standing near her door. The tall thin man looking from clear, blue, gentle eyes behind the spectacles on his face was Sonny's dad.

It came to him in a sweeping gesture of recognition, like awaking from a long, deep sleep and re-entering the world to find it the way you had left it. For one short, bewildering moment, Sonny, his mother, and dad stood there in the surreal moment, as if spell-bound, for none was able to speak. In the very next instant, Sonny and his dad were in each other's arms and weeping. Sonny's mother rose from her desk and ran through the doorway to embrace the two men. The next several minutes were used to wipe at one another's tears and exclaim their shock at being together again, after their resignation to the realities that this moment might never ever happen. With the store now empty, the door was locked and the "Closed" sign was posted in the window. The family huddled in chairs pulled up around the desk in the small back office. Virginia hastily made coffee in a small galley kitchen off the back hallway and returned with a steaming mug for everyone. After putting the coffee on the desk, she could not help throwing her arms around her boy again and kissing his face. As she settled in her chair, the three began sorting out the tragic tangle that had been their lives since Sonny's disappearance.

Later, taken home to his boyhood room, he now lay on the bed, in the cool, calm of the night and thought about all that had happened to him. Both he and his parents had told their full stories to each other, of all they had experienced through these difficult two-and-a-half years. With either a quirk of fate or perhaps something more richly powerful and spiritual, Sonny had been brought to his family's door step. If he hadn't been asked to take Sid's run and come south, none of this would have happened. Yet Sonny felt like God had taken him by the shoulders and literally guided him home. During the afternoon, when he had described for his parents the profound torture he had gone through, not knowing who he was, they shook their heads in disbelief that someone so depraved would rob and leave him for dead.

As the discussion turned to his parents and what they had been through, they asked him if he remembered Gina. At the very sound of her name, it was as if another light turned on in his head. Once again with a flood of emotion he remembered his darling young wife, his soul mate. Sonny's parents shared with him the deep depression that engulfed Gina after his disappearance and then the bomb shell came.

"And you have a beautiful little son named Samuel," said Virginia. Sonny now remembered his wonderful smiling Gina, his very heart. The last night they were together wrapped in each other's arms was the night Samuel was conceived. Now how he longed for her, with an urgent, yet fearful desire. Although his parents had told him Gina had returned to work at the library and was still living at her parents' home, he worried about her reaction at finding he was alive and back in Jesup. Had she forgotten him, the passion and dreams they had shared and moved on with her life? Was there someone else she was now interested in; and if she was, how could he blame her? And a son, he had a son; a stunning truth he had been totally unprepared for.

After breakfast, a nervously excited call was made to Gina in Savannah. It was Sunday morning and the library would be closed, so Gina would be home with Sam. When the phone rang at the Harris's,

Gina picked it up to hear the happy voice of her mother-in-law. After a brief greeting and inquiry about sweet Sam, Virginia said that she had a startling, wonderful surprise for her and asked her to sit down. Gina laughed and asked what on earth Virginia was up to.

"Never you mind," said Virginia "Just do it."

"OK, I am sitting," said Gina, still laughing, wondering what kind of prank Vie had up her sleeve.

"I have someone here that would like to speak to you Gina, now hold on," said Virginia as she handed Sonny the phone.

"Hello darling, it's Sonny," he said.

For a moment there was silence and Sonny wondered if Gina was still on the line, then slowly she said "Sonny, is that really you?"

"Yes, honey it is me," he said. "There is so much I need to tell you, so much has happened to me, to us, when can I see you?" he asked.

After their brief conversation, Gina hung up the phone and stared out the window unable to move. Gina remembered the number of times she had stared out that very same window after Sonny left, praying that the next car to come down the street would carry him back to her, and the total and utter despair she felt as she came to realize he wasn't coming back. Now in a few short hours, he would be here and the thought of it seemed so unreal. Carol looked at Gina and asked if that was Vie on the phone and were they coming over to see Sam, as they often did on weekends. Gina continued to silently stare out the window as if in a trance. Finally, Carol put down the breakfast plate she was washing and stood before Gina with a concerned look on her face.

"What is it?" Carol asked.

Looking up at her mother with tears in her eyes she said, "Mom I just talked to Sonny, he is at home in Jesup."

Arrangements had been made for the Boones to drive up to Savannah that afternoon, arriving around 2:00 p.m. Gina, still in shock, not able to let her emotions go, spent the rest of the morning bathing Sam and putting him in his best rompers, kissing his little man cheeks and tickling him. His happy face squealed with delight and Gina again saw Sonny in his sweet baby smile. Sam was two-and-a-half now and only knew Sonny as a picture on his mother's bedroom dresser. She silently wondered how Samuel, who was usually a happy, friendly boy, would react to meeting his father for the first time. She hoped with all her heart that he would learn to love him as she had, and still did. Then it was her turn to spruce and beautify. Holding her favorite dress up before the mirror, she remembered Sonny loved her in vibrant lavender colors so she pulled it on over her head and smoothed the cotton sheath over her hips. While she checked herself in the mirror again, she realized she was no longer the same young girl Sonny had left standing in the yard so long ago. She had grown up fast and become a mother to her son and was developing a career. And what about Sonny, how might he have changed? The anxiety, fear, and love she felt was all swimming around in her head, along with the butterflies in her stomach.

"Dear God help me through this," she said out loud, to the face that stared back at her from the mirror.

The Boones arrived on time. Carol had fixed some refreshments and was putting napkins out when Art came in to the living room and announced they were here. Gina took Sam's hand as Art answered the door. The first one to enter the room was Sonny. Reaching out to Art for a handshake, Sonny noticed a cool reserve in his response as his questioning eyes searched his own. Carol rushed up to Sonny and hugged him immediately and kissed his cheek saying, "Oh Sonny I just can't believe you are here." Ending the embrace, he looked past Carol and saw Gina for the first time in two-and-a-half years, his eyes fixed on her glowing face. Then his glance dropped to the short little man standing by his mother's side who was smiling. He seemed so happy to be invited to this grown-up party, because Nana had baked his favorite cake.

Gina stood still, staring at Sonny. The very sight of him took her breath away. The moment she had dreamed of during her lonely fitful nights and prolonged empty days of willful desire were fulfilled in that instant, as Sonny slowly crossed the room, searching her teary eyes for the love and longing he himself now felt. As she smiled and dropped Sam's hand to reach for Sonny's open arms, the two embraced in a rapture of sweet innocence, as if for the first time. While they held each other, little Sam moved quickly, laughing, to grab hold of his mother's leg, wanting to play the hug game, too. Sonny's parents embraced each other in tears of joy, while Art and Carol stood holding hands, smiling at their children.

And so it was, that the fortunes of life and the ties that bind, once rent and broken, were finally reconciled. Sonny Boone, a son of the south, had at last found his way home. The bizarre twist of fate that had devastated the lives of these two families, held suspended in their collective pain and loss, were ultimately given solace. In the weeks and months that followed, this young couple put their lives back together and their joy was greater for their loss. Happily, in the center of this merciful, miraculous union sat smiling Sam, the heartbeat of their existence.

Sonny eventually went to work in the family business and later as owner, expanded the operation to include four more stores in the greater Georgia area. Gina had two other children in subsequent years; a daughter Ava, who resembled her and another son, whom they named Thomas, for Father Ed, who had come to Savannah at his birth and also to deliver a letter he had received at the mission from the Army, that had arrived for Sonny just a month after he had returned home. It listed all of his personal information: who he was, where he was born and when, also his parents' names, and where he had entered the service. A mystery solved too late.

Folded in one another's arms, standing on the deck of their Tybee Island home, gazing out over the windswept ocean and the rolling surf; Sonny and Gina watched as their three children chased and play tag among the mounded sand dunes; their sea oat flags fluttering in the breeze. Sonny nuzzled Gina's neck and asked if she remembered their first night together at the beach, on their short honeymoon years ago.

"Yes, I will always remember," she said and he held her closer and kissed her cheek.

Over the joyful laughter of their romping children is the roar of the sea and the never-ending ebb and flow of the tide that continues like the endless stream of humanity. Many souls have passed through this lush sub-tropical realm and have walked over these same cobblestone streets and entered these same iron gates. They have their own legacies and stories to tell. This is one.

Who are the beautiful people and how do they live their privileged lives? Kasandra was one of those people who fit the part that had been written just for her. Beautiful and exotic, she had it all, and was a spectacle of glamour everywhere she went, turning heads and crushing hearts. Enjoy the observation of one who relished it all in **Kasandra**.

KASANDRA

$\mathcal{H}$er slim, long shapely legs were like two sleek bronze runways
that led to well-formed, graceful feet with delicate toes painted with
ruby red lacquer, peeking out of her high-heeled black leather sandals.
But those legs and peek-a-boo toes were not all he noticed about her.
Kasandra, with the exotic sounding name, allowed her head to fall back
on her lounge chair with her face drinking in the sunlight, only partially
blocked by a pair of large black sunglasses with a nest of shimmering
rhinestones gathered at the corners of their shiny frame. The small
symmetrical nose that supported those glasses also sheltered two full,
voluptuous lips below, also ruby, now slightly parted in quiet repose.
Lush, auburn hair flared out from her head against the chair and then
tumbled to her shoulders, brushing her long, exquisite neck as it played
with the breeze. Her slender, well-defined arms stretched forward
comfortably on the curved, bamboo arm rests of her chair with hands
dangling at rest. Could it be she had fallen asleep? Her light silk, polka
dot sun dress caressed her rounded bosom, and hugged her slim waist
and was slightly lifted by the breeze, stirring the gathers of her ruffled
bodice, as she sat so still fixed in the moment. What could he say? She
was the most ravishing thing he had seen lately!

The truth was, from his position at the hotel, he often saw wealthy,
well-groomed, attractive people vacationing in the lush, tropical climes
of his homeland Barbados, a jewel of the Caribbean. Tourism being

the main industry, everyone on the island was involved in one sort of a service job or another. Pampering and pandering to the rich and famous was all in a day's work and how islanders survived. He himself never thought much about living on the scraps that others threw his way. He was just happy for his accommodations that allowed him to enjoy the luxurious ambiance of the spacious veranda with its lavish potted palms, pool, and view of the white, sandy beach and turquoise waters beyond. The dense tropical gardens that surrounded the hotel laden with hibiscus, orchids and giant fern were a particular delight. But with all this said, his eyes wandered back to the vision before him sitting poolside, oblivious to his presence and admiration.

Soon a tall handsome man in white linen slacks and matching shirt wearing a Panama hat sat down beside the beauty and offered her one of the two drinks he carried. In her slow, languorous way, she stretched her sleek feline body as she flashed her companion a seductive smile and reached for a glass. Their heads came together in a conspiratorial mode, when laughter erupted between them. He watched all of this, peeking through thick palm fronds that hid him from view, at the end of the veranda adjacent to the bar where the tall man had picked up his drinks. He observed the interplay between the couple for a while and then as he turned his head to reach for a quick snack, just that fast they were gone. With time on his hands before the evening shift came on, he made a quick appraisal of his own appearance, for it had been a long, hot day.

He scurried over to the side of the pool and refreshed his face in the cool water and rested his hot, tired feet for a few minutes. Next, he looked out over the ocean from the railing around the veranda and noticed that the sky had caught fire again just above the horizon and the North Star pierced the ever-darkening sky. Dusk in this tropical paradise was always spectacular and he never tired of this breathtaking visage of light, color, and shadow. He craned his neck in search of a sliver of silver moon, now only a promise.

In a small alcove off the main kitchen, he took his evening meal that always consisted of salad leavings and bruised, over-ripened fruit. The nice thing was that he never had to make his own meals, they had always been provided; just part of the perks of living at the Royal Palms Hotel. Who could complain about free food served every day as regular as clockwork? It was more than some had and he was grateful. When he finished his last piece of mango, he decided he had just enough time to take a quick stroll in the garden, for then it would be time to get back to the veranda. The elusive fire flies winked and blinked at him as he chased them across the lawn and through the foliage. They teased him for a while then vanished into the upper reaches of the trees. He knew it was a silly game to play, but it made him feel free, alive, and happy.

The veranda at night was a magical place at the Palms. Away from the pool and just off the main luxury dining room were sets of large French doors held opened, leading to an extended section of the terrace flooded with soft, romantic lighting, especially designed for dancing and dining out under the stars. Soft samba music now drifted in the air and mixed rhythmically with the hiss of curling waves being driven by the tide. Palm leaves swayed, rustled by the gentle sea breeze, keeping time with dancers who would lean in then glide on, bathed in the moonlight. Kasandra, now wrapped in the arms of her Latin lover, let the soft chiffon folds of her emerald green gown follow her swaying hips and brush the back of her legs, those fabulous legs. Standing off in the shadows, at the side of the dance floor, he was struck anew with her grace and elegance. After what seemed like hours of feasting and dancing, the handsome young couple headed out for a promenade on the beach. The gentleman lit a cigar and reached for one of Kasandra's hands as she slipped off her shoes and held them with the other. Not being able to help himself, he dashed out to the dunes and crouched behind a stand of sea oats for cover. He felt compelled to see what they might do next.

Now it never occurred to him that his behavior might be misconstrued as voyeurism by some. He preferred to think he had a normal interest and curiosity about people. And so, he peered out from his perch on the dunes and watched Kasandra stroll hand in hand along the windswept beach that night and his heart was glad and his conscience clear. There were others coming and going and he heard their laughter and banter as someone was pushed into the edge of the surf and someone else jogged alone facing the wind. He quietly moved along the ridge of dunes keeping Kasandra in sight. The couple soon stopped walking, and then with their arms stretched around each other, they gazed out on the waves. Slowly the man stole a tender kiss from Kasandra's parted lips, then she leaned her head into his chest and he gently held her there under the stars and moonlight.

The next morning at 11:00 a.m., there was some activity and commotion in the annex to the large dining room. The smaller but beautifully appointed space had been set up for an intimate champagne reception. He stood and looked on from his station near the outside door. To his startling eyes, Kasandra appeared in a sleek, white crepe suite with a large pink orchid pinned to the lapel of her fitted jacket. The strands of pearls at her throat were impeccable and her swept-up hair revealed matching earrings that swung with a modest dangle. She was a glowing apparition and there was a light that shown in her eyes as she looked at her companion, also dressed in a white suit, whom now stood beside her. As guests entered the room, soft music played in the background and the chatter of joy and congratulations filled the air. Kasandra smiled at her friends and held out her left hand as a large diamond ring glittered and was examined by one and all. From the corner of the doorway, he heard an older gentleman laugh and extol the virtues and merits of marriage, a pairing of hearts and souls conjoined as one. Others spoke and all lifted their flutes of champagne in celebration and toasting while waiters circulated with sumptuous trays of tiny morsels to complete the festivities. As occasions went, this kind was always the most interesting and fun to observe. All people being so different, one never knew exactly what to expect. There had after all been that one time when a bride and groom jumped into the pool in full wedding attire and were shortly thereafter joined by all of their guests. The hotel concierge had barely survived that one.

All things taken into account, the past few days had been satisfying on many levels. Other than that narrow escape out of the hotel pool at 4:00 a.m., when six people came in from the beach for an end of evening frolic, he had remained anonymous as far as the hotel guests were concerned. Lucky for him, he was a good swimmer and was able to make it to the edge of the pool and scamper off for cover before anyone noticed him. Breathless, he hid in some foliage, shook his head, and composed himself. The horns on his back were dripping wet and his eyes rotated to miss droplets that ran down his scaly face. Deciding to leave well enough alone, he nestled down in the mulch where he stood and called it a night.

Soon the pink blush of predawn drenched the beach and woke him from his slumber. He heard the familiar rattle and movement of pots and pans coming from the kitchen and slowly moved that direction. His favorite benefactor, Angelo, was moving about preparing a variety of breakfast delights and smiled when he saw him standing in the galley doorway.

Angelo spoke to him as he dropped a scrap of bread for him to sample and asked, "So what are you up to this morning my fine dragon friend?"

As Angelo then stroked his long, barbed tail, he admitted he was the most beautiful iguana he had ever seen. Then by way of a painstaking explanation, Angelo told his reptilian friend that he would have to wait a while for his fruit that morning, for tarts were being prepared right then and coffee had to be made. The iguana bobbed his head up and down and thrust out his colorful throat as a sign of recognition and patience, for he knew what was coming.

In the meantime, at the front of the hotel, the doorman was helping Kasandra and her husband load their luggage into the trunk of a long, black Mercedes sedan with an open sunroof. The two chatted and the man gave the doorman a tip. Smiles were exchanged and farewells made as the excited couple drove around the circled drive and past the spewing fountain that was the centerpiece of the hotel's central garden. The iguana who watched their departure with pleasure and admiration then returned his attention to the galley doorway and matters at hand. Sure enough, laid out in an old pie plate was a mound of banana, mango and persimmons. As the lizard was fed and stroked one more time, he was admonished by Angelo to stay out of trouble that day, and enjoy the beautiful sunshine on the veranda.

Yes, life had been good for this fine, colorful iguana that had been made a pet by the head chief of the hotel some twelve years ago. The once small, immature reptile had happened upon the hotel kitchen door one morning and flashed his most congenial smile upon a man who was emptying trash bins. As fate would have it; it was love at first sight. Angelo and the exotic iguana instantly bonded and as a natural result, the elegant creature had been captivated by people ever since.

Looking over one's shoulder can surprisingly help us move forward in life. The past becomes part for our future and ultimately define who we are. Each person to be savored in their uniqueness defined by laughter, heartache and tears, for such is the substance of life. Pricilla Alcott had a great perspective on things in her small adolescent world and was happy to share her views with anyone who would listen. Enjoy her delightful look back in **Days Remembered.**

DAYS REMEMBERED

I languished in misery that summer as it droned on in the usual way, hot and humid during the day, with sultry, sleepless nights; the old, metal fan on my dresser struggling to move the oppressive, humid air trapped in my small, childhood bedroom. Through the one modest window at the end of my bed, I had often watched the big, bright moon marching its course across the night sky and wondered what the future would hold for me, dreaming of the day when I would be grown. In the heat of summer, crickets, frogs, and katydids sang such a loud, rapturous song, that I imagined they were nestled in the corner of my bedroom putting on a concert for the bed bugs that might have been displaced and climbing on my wall, since mom, in a flurry of cleaning, beat my mattress and rug to a pulp with her spatula. Bed bugs and dust mites beware; she cometh with a vengeance, but I digress.

My name is (Prissy), Pricilla Addison Alcott, but there wasn't really anything prissy about me in those days. You could have asked any of the neighborhood boys about that. I was a glorious thirteen years old at that time, for all the good it did me. I lived in the tiny, backwater town of Parkerville, Georgia, population 3,246 after Grant Henson died that year at the age of 92. It was June 1946 and the adults in my life said that it was time to put the war behind us, pick up our lives and revive this great country of ours. If indeed it was a new day, then why did I feel like a beetle on its back in the noonday sun: hot, hamstrung and hopeless!

Now there was a single narrow ribbon of highway that ran through the heart of our little town, meandering around a big bend then quickly running away through the piney woods on to the next county. The center of our small community consists of six city blocks where all commerce was conducted, offering all the necessities of life as we knew them. For example, there was a drug store with a modest pharmacy in the rear of the building for all that ailed ya, then near the front a tall bar with stools where you could sit and drink an ice-cold Coke for a nickel or have a scoop of ice cream, my personal favorite. There were two small clothing stores in town, but only one that had shoes and they were often in short supply. Gibson's Mercantile was the busiest place on Main Street because it was the only store within 30 miles where you could buy groceries and household items like a broom or pots and pans. Then there was Hodges Barber Shop, Grangers Farm and Feed, and Miss. Nellie Watson's Home Cookin' Café; she did make a mean berry pie. Now the post office, police department and jail were all housed in one building that sat at the end of Fifth Street just across from the gas station. I always thought it was funny how the main road in and out of town was flanked by the jail and gas station. Yeah sorta had your choice; you could fill up and fly, or mess up and lie and hope Ansell Bowdean, the jailer, believed you.

As a thirteen-year-old I was often corrected for having a limited, childlike view on things that the adults around me said would miraculously improve with age. It was solely because of this vexing stage of life where I found myself that I often felt out of sorts. I was no longer considered a child, so I was not allowed to run at will and play with friends, building forts in the woods and skipping rocks in the creek till the sun went down. However, I was not an adult either, so I was not included in certain conversations and activities or confided in with any sort of deference for my priceless opinion. When on occasion I tested the waters by offering my unsolicited advice, I was sharply reprimanded and told not to be precocious! What was a person to do? And what on earth was precocious?

As I sat pouting on the back staircase one night, I overheard my mom in the kitchen explaining my teenage moodiness to my dad. She said I was on the pathway through puberty and that my burgeoning womanhood would very soon be awash in raging hormones that were just ready to explode. My dad, struggling for understanding, made the best analogy he could and compared me to his young heifer in the back pasture that bucked and kicked her heels in the air anytime he came near. A heifer! Can you believe that? And to make matters worse, I was consigned to hard labor that summer; weeding and harvesting the garden was now my responsibility. Picking peas and snappin' beans, then there was shucking corn, cutting rhubarb and pullin' beets. It seemed that my real value was in my strong back and flexible arms that endlessly picked, packed, and bundled the produce from our garden. When I had made the mistake of complaining about this assignment, my father asked me if I would like to continue to eat. Enough said there!

Now according to all the books I was reading in my bedroom at night and the magazines I was consulting, my life paled by comparison to those in the know and on the go. I felt stifled and awkward, like a fish out of water. I too, longed to travel and see the world, have adventures and wear lipstick. Yes, lipstick, hot pink like the blush on a dewy rose. Desperate, I experimented on my own to achieve those rosier lips. By biting my lips, I made them red, then I smeared on some Vaseline to get that glossy look but it wasn't quite the same as what I had seen in the magazines. As a matter of fact, as I came from the bathroom one morning all red and glowing, my mom grabbed hold of me in the hallway. She held me by my cheeks and examined my mouth both inside and out and asked if I was getting a cold sore. Needless to say, that was not the affect I was going for.

Now I must admit, I found myself betwixed and between that summer of '46. For example, one moment I wanted to grab my gear and go play softball, running around those bases like greased lightnin', then skiddin' into home plate in a pile of dust with a hardy "Hi-ho, Silver!" Then a few days later, I would see Jeffry Hodges smiling at me from the third-row pew at church and my stomach would start to flutter for no apparent reason. But I had to give Jeffry credit. For a boy, he was reasonably nice and he sort of had a cute, nervous laugh whenever he said hi to me.

Now you are possibly wondering about my siblings. The truth is, I haven't any. Yes, that's right, I am an only child, the center of my parents' universe, their only hope for the future. I was holding their dreams hostage until fruition, no pressure there. Being an only child can be a good thing and a bad thing. It's a good thing at special times like holidays when you are doted on and there is no one you are expected to share with while being the center of attention; no one to steal your thunder. It is a bad thing when there are chores to be done and there is no one else to help, or even worse, during school days when you are expected to be the family genius.

Then there are those strange moments that come out of the clear blue, like when your mom decides you should take piano lessons, regardless of the fact that your feet don't even reach the peddles and all the keys must be middle "C" because they all look just alike. I still haven't figured that one out. But you know, there were times when I thought I might like a little brother or sister, but then I would get over it pretty quick when I would hear my jealous friends complain about their siblings. No thanks, I decided.

Mmmmm coffee ... there was that entire adult ritual surrounding the preparation and drinking of that dark brown liquid that seemed to have magical powers, for it singlehandedly kept the world a sane place according to my mom and even had the ability to jump start most mornings when no one wanted to get out of bed. For as far back as I can remember, that familiar rich aroma of brewing coffee has greeted me each morning, as if that wonderful smell was tugging at the edge of my blanket and nudging me to wake up and greet the day. As a young child, I would slowly creep down the stairs each morning and poke my head around the kitchen door. I always saw two sleepy-eyed parents shuffling around in their pajamas yawing and groaning as they reached for that first cup of coffee with its lifesaving jolt. After a second cup, I could almost be assured that life would go on as usual and eventually the thought of food would enter their minds. Every now and then if I got up fairly early, while mom and dad were still having coffee hour, they would occasionally invited me to join them and would offer me a cup of warm sweet milk with a dash of coffee in it. I was told to sit quietly and not to speak or make any early morning demands. On those rare occasions, I remember feeling very grown up and included with a real sense of belonging as the three of us sat there in the silence embracing our mugs. At the age of thirteen, I had my very own coffee cup and was allowed a few extra dollops of coffee to my warmed milk whenever I wanted but the rule for silence remained the same ...shush!

Clarice Williams was our black cleaning lady, who helped Mom with chores in the house and the laundry on wash day. She had a one-year-old baby boy named Abner, who was as sweet as slow molasses. Every time he'd see me, he would light up and throw his chubby little arms out wide for me to grab him. His big, round dark brown eyes just sparkled and his cheeks puffed out when he smiled and laughed. Abner usually played on the floor in the kitchen while Clarice folded laundry and ironed clothes. Sometimes I was allowed to take Abner out for a stroll in the yard where I would show him the flowers, trees, and point up at the big blue sky. Abner gurgled and cooed when you talked to him and would pat his tiny little hands together with excitement and that made us both laugh. Mama said all babies were a wonder and a precious gift from God. Clarice's husband was killed in the last year of the war and the pain, fear, and loss she felt so overwhelmed her that she was unable to speak or come out of her house for two weeks. Finally, people at her church and in the neighborhood coaxed her along and back to life. Mom tended her some and eventually she came back to work. Precious little Abner would never know his daddy but was sure enough loved by his mama.

I always looked forward to the Fourth of July. That year, Independence Day seemed to be anticipated in a more reverent and heartfelt way because of the end of the war and all the many lives that had been altered by it forever. Everyone was so excited about our small-town parade. Many got to town early that day to set up their favorite spot by the roadside. Dad had decorated his flatbed hay wagon with a paper skirt of red, white and blue and was to pull his wagon of returned veterans down through the center of town, just behind the county high school marching band. Next in line would be the Jeep posse led by the sheriff and jailer who would toss out saltwater taffy to the kids along the way. A few farmers who owned horses formed the honor guard. With their flags pointed forward, draped in the morning sun, Old Glory, the American flag was front and center and flanked by our state and county flags. Many were emotional that day and clapped, yelled and whistled as the colors passed by. The horses whinnied and bobbed their heads as they danced along the pavement to the beat of distant drums.

To me the very best part of the celebration was all the food and mountains of it. Mom would make piles of crispy fried chicken, a huge potato salad and a few dozen deviled eggs. Aunt Leah, mom's sister and all of her family would be over about noon and she would bring coleslaw, homemade yeast rolls and a chocolate devil's food cake slathered in deep curls of rich frosting. Uncle Frank, dad's bachelor brother always brought the watermelon and lemonade. That year, the Peterson Clan from across the street, who were new in town, had been invited as well. They had five young boys from ages two to ten starting with Delbert who was the oldest, then Julian, and Norman, then Billy and Sims, rascals one and all, but lots of fun. The eatin' would commence at 12:00 p.m. and would not let up until utter collapse and the sun went down. As the day finally faded, there would be fabulous fireworks, those glorious star bursts high in the sky, and we kids would chase each other through the yard with swirling sparklers as the adults watched from their chairs on our big, deep porch. Then as tradition always dictated, Dad and Uncle Frank would light up their Fourth of July cigars, sing a few patriotic songs and praise God for the freedoms we enjoy as Americans. "Oh, say can you see..." What a day!

Have I mentioned that a branch of the Savannah River runs through Parkerville, where the town fathers built a small city park many years back? There were several picnic benches spread along the shoreline under a grove of elm, sycamore, and oak trees and there was a large sandbar that made a perfect beach for swimming. An ancient oak tree draped with Spanish moss hung out over the river. It had an old tire swing attached by a rope tied to its branches. Many a hot summer day was lulled away with swimming and pushing off the tire swing to make a huge ark out over the water, then gleefully releasing the rope while flying through the air to make a giant splash in the cool, deep water below, the largest splash always in dispute.

Now there was that one time when Jimmy Johnson ran to the shore of the river laughing as he skipped along, kicking up the water as high as he could. In the froth of the waves, he did not see a water moccasin he had disturbed. All of the sudden there was a blood curdling scream that caught everyone's attention. As we all looked to see what was going on, we saw Jimmy dancing around in the shallow water with a six-foot snake hanging onto his foot. We instantly all jumped out of the water and rushed toward Jimmy who was by then slumped on the shore rubbing his foot, the snake having slithered away. Jimmy, trying not to cry, yelled for someone to run and get help. Amy Tyler jumped on her bike and peddled as fast as she could to the police station just two blocks away to get the sheriff.

Now the only kind of emergency medical help we had in our small town in those days was Henry Tate. He had been an Army corpsman several years back and was then retired. When he moved to town several years earlier, he remodeled his garage to make a medical treatment room where he offered first aid to the people of our community, until they could be seen at the county medical center over in Jesup some twenty-seven miles away. When the sheriff arrived on the scene that day, he had already called Jimmy's parents and then scooped the boy up in his arms and rushed him over to Henry's with red lights and sirens blaring on his police car.

When Henry looked at Jimmy he could see a massive, red swollen area on the side of his left foot and Jimmy was feeling pretty shaky like he might even throw up. Henry cleansed the wound and gave Jimmy a tetanus shot and told his parents to get him over to the county center as soon as possible. The sheriff led the way with his lights and sirens on, while Jimmy and his parents followed in their car close behind as they all rushed out of town. Well, it was a few days later when we all heard the news that Jimmy was fine because he had been given some anti-venom serum at the medical center and had stayed there overnight just to make sure he was out of the woods. You can be sure after that we all had a more watchful eye when we splashed and played in our favorite summer fun spot.

Everyone needs and usually has a best friend growing up, someone special to share secrets with, someone who will always be there for you through thick and thin. That someone for me was Carol Henley. We were both hometown girls with that deep red Georgia clay between our toes and a genealogy that stretched back to the Civil War. Carol and I met in first grade over at the county primary and middle school in Tyler and have been close friends ever since. My home in town was about a mile from the small farm where Carol lived. Over the years we established many bike trails between our homes that skirted fertile pastures, meandered through pine and oak wood forests, and roamed across beautiful open meadows. We had secret hiding places along the way where we would meet to talk, have snacks and make plans. It was at one of our favorite places, at the base of a huge oak tree on the edge of the woods we called the hollow, that we met one lazy Saturday afternoon, a rendezvous that I will never forget.

We had started out by looking at movie magazines, then moved on to the latest hairstyles and discussed the necessary evils of zit cream. Soon, Carol got a mischievous look on her face and began to laugh. When I asked what was funny, she produced from her jacket pocket, two cigarettes and a blue plastic lighter.

"Oh man," I said. "Where did you get those?"

She made a daring smirk and said she had lifted them from a pack her dad had left out on their back porch and had raided his stash of lighters in a kitchen drawer. After handing me one, she made a dramatic pose and asked if she looked like Lauren Bacall and I quickly assured her that she did. We both proceeded to put a cigarette between our lips and decided they didn't taste very good. Carol then suggested that the full-bodied flavor would probably be released when we fired them up. She lit hers first, drew in a large deep breath then let it out choking. While gagging and laughing at the same time she reached over to light mine. Soon the two of us were in a spasm of choking and laughter we could hardly control, all the time posing for one another as we had seen done in the movies. Then it happened, I looked up and saw a farmer crossing his field with rubber boots on and a shovel tossed over his shoulder. He was out checking his irrigation ditch that ran along the edge of the woods. He was headed our way. We panicked. Not wanting to get caught smoking, we madly gathered up our magazines, threw down the cigarettes and ran deeper into the woods as fast as our skinny, short legs would carry us.

Finally reaching what we thought to be a safe distance, we stopped running, caught our breath and looked back over our shoulders. To our shock and horror, we saw a fire blazing at the base of our special oak tree. As we crouched low behind some shrubs, we saw the farmer yelling to someone and soon two men were there beating back the flames at the edge of the woods with the back of their shovels. Black smoke billowed from the dry leaves and pine needles that ignited into flames from our carelessly discarded cigarettes. Thank goodness the two farmers working in their field that day were able to put out the fire before it got out of control. By then, we had all the excitement we could stand for one day and so decided to go our separate ways, but only after making a solemn pledge to one another to never mention the smoking incident again and the day we nearly set the woods on fire.

There were many other events that happened that summer, highlighting that extraordinary time in my life. It was a year of many firsts for me. As a young girl struggling within her cocoon of adolescence to flower into a young lady with all the attributes of womanhood, I often felt a bit frightened, confused and terribly excited all at once. As I began to more closely observe the women in my life, I found much to emulate and in return received needed assurance from them, that I was totally normal and that all would be well, if you know what I mean.

I will never forget the day mom introduced me to something she called a training bra that further disturbed my sense of self. I remember thinking it odd that one's own chest needed some sort of training. I finally concluded that it was just one more of those mysteries about being a female I would need to learn more about. Slowly, over time, I was being introduced to an entire world of under garments that were supposed to enhance one's stature and natural beauty while being practical for all sorts of things like holding up socks and keeping your tummy flat. Who knew those kinds of things were important?

As a matter of fact, one of those contraptions looked like a sling shot with arms like an octopus that was used to clip on stockings. Mom called it a garter belt. The last straw that further complicated my life that summer was the Sunday afternoon Mom and Aunt Leah decided I should have my first perm to fluff my hair and give it body. Well, I cried for the next several weeks, not wanting to come out of my room, because of the crown of bed springs that covered my head. They could not be managed or restrained by any amount of brushing, clipping up with barrettes, or pushing back with headbands. My hair was frizzed and I looked like I had put my finger in an electrical socket. Thanks, Mom!

Looking back, I have to smile and even laugh remembering that tumultuous summer of '46. Who was that little button of a girl, who watched the big, bright moon in the starry sky, who dreamed of the day when she would be grown? Now sitting bent with age in my wheelchair near the fire, as the silent snow blankets the landscape beyond my window, I am like the dying embers I see before me. However, I am filled with the sweetness of love and gratitude for the rich, wondrous life I have lived and for all those who came and went, gracing my existence like a rich tapestry of textures and color. I now look to the future with great hope and joy, for soon my real life begins. I will embrace eternity shrouded in beauty, perfection, and glory. So, goodnight (Prissy) Pricilla Addison Alcott ... sleep tight and do not let the bed bugs bite.

Carly Atkins was a woman with a purpose, fully devoted to her art career; that is until Justin Russo stumbled into her life. She never knew love could feel so great or cause so much pain. Things are not always what they appear to be on the surface. **Out of the Shadows** tells her story.

OUT OF THE SHADOWS

$\mathcal{T}$here had been that special moment in time as a young girl when she just knew destiny had whispered her name. Her cluttered art shop that held the focus of her life was littered with the expressions of her passion that bled through her work and into her personal life. Carly Atkins had found herself as a young woman, totally immersed in the Art Nuevo and Art Deco movements of the 1920s and 30s when she moved to South Beach, Florida. As the only child of a New York stock broker and mother of the social registry of Atlantic City's famous Boardwalk Hotels, her privileged yet sterile upbringing in the best girls' schools in the East changed dramatically when, at the age of nineteen, she began attending the National Academy School of Fine Arts in New York City. The times were fraught with peril, especially for a young girl sheltered and isolated from the realities of life by power and wealth. Hem lines had been raised, women were smoking cigarettes in public and everyone was listening to jazz and dancing the Charleston while consuming hidden flasks of cheap contraband gin forced by Prohibition. The stock market rose and fell in rhythmic volatility making some millionaires and others paupers overnight. The times were ripe for ruin and many found their way to the road of no return.

Carly, from her earliest childhood, had shown an interest in and talent for the visual arts. Her favorite medium was oil paint, the rage in her day that had found a footing in many of the new artistic expressions like impressionism. Over the years of her private schooling, she had opportunities to exhibit her talent, painting backdrops for annual school plays, entering district art shows and providing artwork for her school's literary magazine. Because of her wonderful talent and desire to become a professional artist, her parents had condescended to allow her to apply at the National Academy because of its high standard of excellence, only exceeded by Julliard for the Performing Arts. An adequate degree of snob appeal concerning the school's exclusivity and past notables that were now being collected, had provided just enough cache` to the academy's reputation for Carly's parents to support her application.

During her twenties, she had explored new ways to define herself through her work. The naturalistic themes of Art Nuevo captured her interest, for it was a wonder world apart from the rude, crude rush of the times, so it helped keep her grounded in life as she knew it. But it wasn't long before the intensity of the changing world around her began to breach the barriers she tried so hard to sustain. Her fellow students teased her unmercifully about her prudish tendencies and what they perceived as a total lack of sophistication. She had gone out on a few dates from time to time with young men in her classes, but found most of them to be too introspective and self-absorbed or lax and irresponsible.

Finally, when she finished her training she quickly packed her bags along with her art supplies and flew to Miami, Florida, the tropical paradise she visited while vacationing as a child and a hot bed for artists of every persuasion. There were novelists, playwrights, painters and musicians. After moving into a loft studio apartment, she connected with a local gallery that agreed to hang a few pieces of her work on a trial basis. She then launched into her craft with a vengeance, often painting until the wee hours of the morning, then crashing on her cot, wrapping herself into an old shawl she had picked up at a street market. Her happiness centered on her work in those days and the singular, simple lifestyle she had carved out for herself.

One Tuesday morning as she rushed inside a local bookstore to get out of the rain, she noticed a young man seated in one of the reading chairs with a stack of books on his lap, a pencil clutched between his teeth, pulling a small notebook from his pocket. He looked a bit harried until he saw Carly staring at him, then he removed the pencil from his mouth and smiled.

Carly, flush with embarrassment, darted between two stacks of books and pretended to be looking intently for an elusive volume of nothing in particular while it poured outside. Soon she peeked out between the shelves to see if the pencil biter was still in his seat and to her regret he was not. As she backed up and returned to the stack of books before her, she bumped into the young man as he was now standing right behind her. With the same grin on his face, he inquired if she was finding what she was looking for. Embarrassed for her deception of jumping into the store to get out of the storm, she smiled back and said, "Oh yes, thank you."

The young man let out a little chuckle as he noticed the title of the book she placed back on the shelf, *The Dinosaur Diaries* by Milton Upps. "Are you a paleontologist then?" he asked with a laugh. This time Carly smirked as well, for she realized she had been found out.

The young man informed her that his name was Justin Ramano, and that he managed the bookstore part-time while finishing a degree in engineering at the Miami University. She shared with him her adventures in the art world and they laughed about the fact that she had never even painted a dinosaur. Justin asked if Carly was a coffee drinker and she held that thought a moment as she looked him over. He had a handsome face with wonderful, large brown eyes that seemed to glisten with mischief. She had always been drawn to beautiful eyes. His manner was light and easy and she liked that too. She grinned at him and asked if he was inviting her to have coffee. He replied that she was a very perceptive girl and asked if she was giving him a yes as he offered her his arm. Laughing at his gallant gesture, she took his arm and he led her out the front door of the bookstore under the cover of his large, black umbrella that was stationed by the door.

They dashed half a block and entered a small bakery that smelled divine with the rich aroma of coffee and delightful confections of every kind. Taking a small table near the front window, they settled into their chairs and Justin asked her what she fancied. Sometime later as they finished their second cup of Columbian blend and wiped at their mouths after enjoying the last bites of their peach tarts, they looked at one another with delight for this chance meeting. Through their conversation, they came to realize they shared some similar interests. They both loved canoeing, cooking, and books. They had discussed their ambitions concerning their future careers and what they hoped would be the fruition of their dreams. When they parted company outside the

185

bakery that day, Justin asked if he could call on Carly sometime, so she jotted her address down on Justin's small notepad. Such were the casual beginnings of what turned out to be a watershed moment in Carly's life, a time that would define her for years to come. For this innocent first encounter, that on the surface seemed ordinary in every way, held a harbinger of emotional turmoil that she could never have conceived.

After several months of quiet walks along the beach and long conversations, late night dinners at one of their apartments, along with art shows, concerts, and readings, Carly and Justin become the closest of friends and found a comfort and joy in one another that seemed so natural. However, they both sensed that their relationship had begun to take a turn. Justin, over time, had slowly reached inside Carly's timid heart and touched her soul, blessing her with his own unique strengths and vulnerabilities that she found irresistible and intoxicating. During profound moments of shared longing, their passions had grown.

One night, Justin arrived at Carly's apartment for dinner but was unusually late. His demeanor was brutish and troubling when he arrived. Carly asked if there was anything wrong, but Justin just paced up and down nervously saying it would all work itself out. Carly tried to calm Justin by handing him a glass of iced tea and urged him to sit at the table to eat something. After she served their plates, Justin tried to smile and make light of the situation but Carly saw that he was merely pushing his food around on his plate. He finally gave up the pretense of eating and placed his napkin on the table and stood up.

"Carly, I have to fly to Chicago in the morning and I am not sure how long I will be gone," he said.

She looked surprised and asked what the trip was about, but he declined to give any details. He said it was just a business trip and he hoped to be back in a week. As she pressed him for more information he simply grabbed his jacket, gave her a quick kiss on her cheek, told her goodbye and was out the door before she knew what had happened. Carly had never seen Justin like this before and worried he might be in some kind of trouble.

As Justin settled into his seat for his flight to Chicago, he glanced out the window and felt pangs of guilt about Carly and the way he had behaved at her apartment. He hated that he was so abrupt with her and had no doubt left her upset and confused. But he just didn't know what else he could have done under the circumstances. He surely could not tell her the truth, at least not now. The trouble was, he never planned to fall in love. He was just a semester away from graduating and had already lined up some lucrative opportunities to launch his career and then he was blindsided by this beautiful, sensitive artistic creature from out of nowhere, who oddly enough seemed to be drawn to him in the same way. And then there was the ever present other, his family and the reason for this emergency trip. While the plane climbed to cruising altitude, Justin reflected on his family and what he would do and say when he arrived in Chicago. He thought this nightmare had ended when he moved to Florida a few years back and decided on a new path for his life but the ties that bind had been stronger and more compelling than he had imagined. Had he really been so naive as to believe they would just let him walk away?

When Justin reached the curb in the pick-up area of Chicago's O'Hare airport, his father's black Lincoln was there waiting for him. Tedo, his father's chauffer waved to him and came to place his bags in the trunk. While they pulled away from the curb, Justin turned toward Tedo and asked "How are things?"

"Not good, Tedo, replied but it will be better now that you are here." After a short drive through the suburbs, the Lincoln turned up Riverside Drive and through the iron gates that kept the residence secluded. Justin felt a wave of anxiety sweep over him at the very sight of his boyhood home that would have been a happy nostalgic moment for most other young men returning after years away.

The minute Justin entered the foyer of the house with Tedo who carried his bags, his mother Maureen, called out his name and appeared from the kitchen wiping her hands on a tea towel. She instantly rushed to put the towel aside and with a warm but tired smile spread her arms wide exclaiming that she thought she heard someone come in. Embracing her son, she clung to his neck and whispered she was so glad he had come home because she really needed him at a time like this.

The Romano family had immigrated from Sicily in 1897 and made their way to Chicago, Illinois, by train where they were greeted by extended family members and friends that had launched out a decade earlier. Theodore Romano, Justin's grandfather, was an imposing figure at six feet tall. He was thick like a wrestler, sporting a heavy, black mustache and full head of wavy hair that bushed out around his broad face. He was tall and stocky for a Sicilian and as strong as an ox. He became employed at the Chicago stockyards doing menial labor at first, but before long had parlayed himself into a position as a distribution manager at an affiliated warehouse. As time moved on, Theo came to have three sons, Antonio, Carlo and Dominick, who was Justin's father. In turn, all three of Theo's sons went to work with their dad. Soon, other ways to make a dollar became more enticing and lucrative. So the Romano boys gravitated to bribery, extortion, and gambling as a means of employment. What started out slowly as side attractions for extra cash, over time became a syndicate, the Romano Family business. Romano Distributors Inc. became a front for their underworld operation.

Justin kissed his mother, then she led him to the kitchen where she had prepared all of his favorite dishes, just as any good Italian mama would. She insisted that he sit and eat before unpacking. Justin loved his mother and had great compassion for the long years she worked so hard to keep her family together, and protected under extraordinary pressures from within and outside the family circle. But it seemed to Justin, that in spite of all her best efforts and good intentions, the drama of their lives over the years had culminated into this threshold moment of pain and shock that could not be denied. As Justin sat alone with his mother in the afternoon twilight of her kitchen, she filled Justin in on the details of what was happening with Romano Distributors Inc., its CEO Dominick Romano Justin's father and his two family partners, Angelo and Marco Romano who were Justin's two older brothers.

Extortion and racketeering as a vocation do not come without risks. And no matter how well calculated or nuanced a deal might be, there is always the potential for things to go south, in this case on the south side of Chicago, on a dark, rainy night, at a warehouse on the corner of Seventh and Hampton.

Dominick and Marco had arranged to meet with the leadership of a rival organization to discuss a turf controversy. The two top leaders and their perspective seconds met at 10:00 p.m. But as is often the case, there was no honor among thieves that night and the cards were stacked against Dominick and Marco as they walked into an ambush. Marco was brutally beaten and left for dead. Dominick was shot twice in the chest and killed.

This gangland-style murder of a major player rocked Chicago's underworld and further reprisal was expected. Marco was clinging to life in a metro hospital with extensive wounds to his vital organs. Although they hoped he would live, no one could predict what life might hold for him moving forward. A funeral for Dominick had been hastily put together for the following day, with only family and close friends expected to attend.

Maureen held Justin's hand and patted it as she looked imploringly into his eyes and said, "I am so sorry for all of this," her voice strained with emotion. "I have sensed for some time now," Maureen said, " that Dominick was in over his head and in real trouble but of course he would tell me nothing." She went on to explain that with Marco in critical condition in the hospital, it would fall to Angelo to keep things going. Shaking her head, she reminded Justin that as much as she loved her son, they both knew Angelo had no leadership skills or the respect and support of those around him at the business. Angelo had always been spoiled and arrogant, attitudes he flaunted in the face of others for years. Now that loyalty and camaraderie were needed, they seemed to be in short supply. Maureen turned away from Justin and walked to the kitchen sink, gazing out the window to the expansive garden beyond. After a brief silence, while both were caught up in their own thoughts, Maureen slowly turned and looked at her son, tears swimming in her eyes and said, "We so need you here now. What is to become of us?"

Later on that night, Justin met with his brother Angelo behind closed doors in their father's study. The two brothers hugged, a family formality, then Angelo collapsed in a leather chair by the unlit fireplace and began to web his fingers together, shaking his head in total disbelief that the repercussions of his shallow, wasted, corrupt life had come home to roost.

"What are we going to do Justin?" asked Angelo. "The word is they have a contract out on both of us." Justin stood beside his brother and looked down on him with contempt.

"I have never wanted anything to do with this business," Justin said. "I thought I made that pretty clear and I refuse to be swept into this nasty mess that has no bearing on me or the life I live." He went on emphatically, "I am telling you one more time Angelo, that I will have no part of this beyond seeing that our mother is provided for."

As he began to walk away, Angelo simply replied, "You're in it whether you like it or not!"

The next morning, Justin went to see his brother Marco in the hospital. The hallway in front of his room was crowded with officials. He was identified as one of the Romano boys through a photograph produced by an FBI agent and forced to sign in for a visitor's pass. They were documenting everyone who even came near Marco. Once inside the dimly lit room, Justin slowly walked to Marco's bed side, overcome by the sight of all the tubes and bandages holding him together. Marco lay there unconscious with his eyes closed; his precarious life hanging by a thread. Pulling up a chair, Justin sat alone in the silence. Soon his face fell into his hands and he wept for the first time.

In his anguish he cried out, "Dear God, how has it all come to this?" Deep down inside, of course, he knew full well how all this had come to pass. That is why as a teenager, he began the process of separating himself from the family, plotting an escape as it were. He realized even then that his father, with the help of his two brothers, was running a criminal enterprise. They had a total disregard for the law and what was ethically right or wrong and certainly never worried about who might get hurt in the process. Pride, greed and a pseudo sense of manly bravado were the driving forces behind Romano Distributors Inc. The wealth that was generated by their nefarious dealings produced a sense of grandeur and entitlement that was icing on the cake. Yes, they had thought themselves indestructible, until now. As Justin checked his watch, he realized it was time to leave for his father's funeral.

A full week passed and Carly hadn't heard from Justin. She spent sleepless nights and days of agitation worrying about him. The hours came and went and still no word. Even her work had suffered as she fell behind on two commissions she had taken. She couldn't seem to focus on her life at hand because, like it or not, she came to acknowledge how Justin had become the grounding center of her existence. Without him she was set adrift and lost in her distress and fear. After three weeks turned into four, she reconciled that she might never see Justin again and her anguish was almost unbearable. Her shattered heart found no solace in her work and she kept asking herself, *could she have been wrong about Justin?* That was the question that plagued her days and continued to wet her pillow at night. Carly turned to the Lord, fervently praying for Justin's safety and return. She felt that she was operating in the dark, knowing nothing of the true circumstances of Justin's disappearance but trusted that the God who knows all, would find him and keep him safe. As time went on, Carly leaned on God more and more for the strength and courage she did not possess.

One week later, it was midnight when the phone rang next to the chair Carly was slumped in, asleep, her Bible still in her hand. After the third ring, she roused herself and answered in a sleep filled, groggy voice.

"Carly, it's me Justin," came a voice on the line. "Carly, I need to see you and explain, so much has happened to me," he said.

"Is it really you Justin? Where are you?" she replied.

"Yes, honey it's me, I just got back in town and I know it's late but I have to see you, can I please come by?" Carly bit her lip hard to keep from crying over the phone, then finally managed to tell him to come. She put some coffee on to brew and grabbed a quick shower, all the time, hoping she had not imagined Justin's call. When the doorbell rang, she let out a sigh of relief and opened the door.

There he stood looking somewhat worse for the wear, but nonetheless, there he was and the moment Carly saw him she rushed into his arms. Once inside the apartment, she took his hands and held him at arm's length to really look him over. He had bruises on his handsome face and a five o'clock shadow she had rarely seen. Wide-eyed, she surveyed his rumpled appearance while dozens of questions swirled through her mind. Finally she asked, "What has happened to you?"

They spent the early hours of the morning huddled around the coffee pot in Carly's kitchen, as she listened intently while Justin described the ordeal he had been through over the past few weeks. The grim confession concerning his family and the horror of what had happened to them was the most difficult admission he had ever made. He loved Carly with an intensity he had never experienced before and realized that in this moment of truth, he could lose her forever. But he was tired of running and lying to cover up his shame. He had to tell Carly the whole truth, if they were to have any chance at a future together, so he recounted all of the hideous events as he remembered them.

After Dominick was laid to rest, it wasn't a week later that Marco succumbed to a raging infection and renal failure. He died alone in the early hours of the morning in his hospital bed with no family there to note his passing. After putting Marco in the ground, there were terrible fights and arguments with Angelo who became more distraught and irrational by the day. The business was floundering and several of the long-time loyalists walked out on Angelo. Only a few remained on the fringes, full of self-interest, to jockey for position on a sinking ship. One night, Angelo was in his father's study going over some paperwork and drinking heavily. He was arguing with his mother about expenses and Maureen was tearful and terrified, pleading with him to calm down and stop drinking.

Justin and Angelo got into a fierce argument that broke out into a fist fight. Suddenly Angelo darted to his father's desk and pulled a gun from the top drawer. Wildly brandishing the pistol in the air, he hollered out abusive, drunken threats. Justin screamed for his mother to get out of the room and as she fled in sheer panic, Justin suddenly lunged at Angelo. While they struggled over the gun, it discharged, sending a bullet into a draped window across the room shattering its glass. Screams and cries could be heard from Maureen as she dashed into the hallway. Through the scuffle, Angelo lost control of the gun and managed to get to his feet. Half crazed, he staggered to a nearby cabinet seizing a bottle of scotch and ran from the house with the bottle tucked under his arm. He peeled out of the driveway in his sleek black sports car then sped down Riverside Drive and out of sight. Early the next morning, there were two policemen at the front door wanting to verify the identification of a Mr. Angelo Romano, who had plowed his car into the oncoming traffic on Highway 56 at 4:00 a.m. that morning. Devastated beyond endurance by the heavy gruesome losses in her family, Maureen fell into Justin's arms and wept inconsolably.

Completely shattered and unable to cope, Maureen was sent to California to live with her sister for a while. It was finally Justin that stood alone at the house the day the real estate man put his sign in the yard then drove away. Locking the front door behind him, Justin walked to his rental car then turned to look up at the house one last time, his heart choked with sadness and regret for all that might have been. As he drove through the iron gates of the estate late that afternoon, he reflected on the irony that those who had lived by the sword had ultimately died by the sword. He remembered the anonymous phone call he received telling him he was no longer a hunted man by the mob as long as he was never seen or heard from again, but he very much felt like a haunted man, aching inside, longing to shed the ghosts of his past.

Justin trembled as he reached across the table and took Carly's hand, his eyes swimming with emotion. She had truly been stunned by these revelations, hardly knowing how to respond. But when he searched her eyes, he sensed her heart was full of mercy and compassion. Carly soon got up from the table and moved behind Justin while he sat in his chair and she encircled him in the warmth of her embrace. As she nuzzled him close, she whispered in his ear that she loved him deeply and dearly because she had only known him as a man of character and integrity and that the knowledge of his secret past could die with her.

A Postscript:

With the past finally reconciled, one year later Carly and Justin were married at a beautiful church on a sun-drenched day in Miami. Justin had finished his degree and was starting a new job with a major construction firm building expensive luxury hotels along Miami's famous beachfront, resort property like the famous Alexander Hotel. The nuptial was attended by the young couples' friends and families. Carly's mother and father had flown in from New York and thought it priceless that Carly had married a man in the hotel business that her mother was so familiar with, for the fabulous Marlborough Blenheim in Atlantic City was owned by her family. Justin flew his mother in from California and she looked healthier and stronger than she had in years. Maureen was so delighted to meet Carly, the center of her son's heart, and pressed a lovely gold broach in her hand at the reception, an heirloom Maureen's mother had brought from Italy years before. It was truly clear through all that had happened, God's grace, redemption and restoration were possible, especially for those who desperately seek it. For out of the ashes of ruin hope still abounds.

A *Tiny Tickler Bonus Story*: what can go wrong when you put a Scottish farmer in a gated retirement community in Florida? Read **Behind the Gate** to find out.

BEHIND THE GATE

$\mathcal{D}$onald Ross was a fine Scottish gentleman with an even temperament and earthly sensibilities. He had been raised on the land after all and as a natural course developed a keen love for animal husbandry and the like. Even though he had lived in America for several years, he was schooled in and held an affection for his Scottish heritage and as a result had made several trips to the old homeland over the years. For decades, he had participated in the Scottish American community and had done all he could to provide funds and ingenuity to help organize the Scottish Highland Games held throughout the Southeastern states every year. The games host such odd events as the sheath toss, where one forks a large bale of hay and pitches it over the back of the shoulder as far as one can for a distance record, then there's the boulder toss which is self-explanatory, and the Caber toss, turning what looks like a telephone pole, end over end for a distance score. It goes without saying that a certain amount of girth is required of each participant. It would seem to the outsider that the ancient Celts had an odd adaptation to the sporting world and in that notion, they would be right. And then there is the whole other issue of the bag pipes. The high-pitched whine and drone of what some have laughingly called a cat in a bag. It is indeed a strange looking instrument, resembling an octopus, with its bag and various tentacle like appendages that yelp when squeezed properly. Oh, but how its evocative notes stirs the heart of the Highlander.

On occasion, Donald Ross was known to cut quite a figure as a kilted man in his day; proudly adorned in the ancient plaid of the Ross clan, with his short, cut-away fine wool field jacket and sporran, a pouch worn in front at the waist to carry supplies such as tobacco, money and the keys to the BMW. The formal attire is a variation on a theme, with the same kilt, but now sporting a Bonnie Prince Charles short, black dress jacket that may be worn with a cummerbund and bow tie if needed. It was at such moments of formality that Flora, Donald's beloved wife, would swoon like a school girl, marveling at her luck to have the affections of such a man, whom she often referred to as her Norse God.

At the mature age of eighty-four, Donald found himself no longer able to manage a large property with extensive gardens and animals to tend. It was then that he traveled to Florida, to reside in a retirement community. He would spend the rest of his days in quiet repose, tending his potted plants on the extended lanai and visiting with his son the Piper as they reminisced about his last trip to Old Scotia. But can you ever really take the Highlander farm boy out of the man and tuck it away behind the iron gates of a retirement community without repercussions.? Can the kilt be hung in the back of the closet along with all that he ever was and adapt him to his new surroundings, the place where life had led him? That indeed was the question to be answered, and where our story begins.

As Donald and Flora were out in their very small yard one morning, having finally straightened out their house from the move, they turned their attention to the neglected flower bed just beyond their patio. Reaching for their coffee cups, they gazed at the perimeter of their new "estate." They had exchanged their acres for a postage stamp that snuggly surrounded their duplex condo, like a fat lady in a girdle hoping to contain her splendor without spilling over. Yes, their new accommodations were nice, clean, and just large enough to contain their favorite furnishings, yet small enough to be quite manageable for two people in their later years. But with all that said, as they sipped their coffee that morning, they wondered about the prospects for their new life that was going to take some getting used to.

"So what with all the rain" said Flora, "I do believe we could graze sheep in the side yard, the grass has grown so tall."

"Aye, it has," said Donald, now swallowing the dregs of his cup and motioning for Flora to refill it, which she dutifully does from her sideboard on the patio.

Flora then sat down beside her dear husband, on their iron glider with the bright orange cushions, and as he gently rocked her he inquired, if he were to buy her a sheep to graze the side yard, what kind would she like?

Playing with him, for she couldn't resist, she said, "Well a Dartmoor of course." At this pronouncement he patted her on the knee and said, "That's a mighty fine choice, but I might have to go all the way to Devon, England, to find one, because they have become so scarce." They sipped at their coffee and chuckled at their nonsense as they glided back and forth, each now deep in their own thoughts. The flower bed went without weeding; perhaps another day.

Now a quick word on the Dartmoor Sheep. The extra wooly creature has the look of a shag rug on legs. It is furry to the extreme; so much so, that its modest head all but disappears in the fluff. When full grown, it is the size of a standard collie. They are known to out-produce wool by any other breed, the quality of their wool being superior. This breed of sheep hails from Devon, England, where they are now locally managed by an association of growers, for they have been placed on the endangered species list. So as Donald sat on the glider that bright, summer morning, he thought to himself what a fine sheep the Dartmoor is and how he would still like to have one; and that is where the trouble begins.

As the weeks came and went and the summer waned on, one morning Flora, after a strenuous round of housekeeping, poured herself a glass of iced tea and headed to the patio for a rest. It is then she notices for the first time that her dear husband, who has been missing in action for the better part of the morning, is now in the far corner of the backyard, working on some type of construction project. Curiosity getting the better of her, she sauntered across the lawn and asked Donald what he was doing. With a prideful grin on his manly, whiskered face he replied he was building an enclosure for a wee garden plot. He then pointed to several pots of veining jasmine and said that when they spread, they will completely cover the outside of his structure and no one will even realize that it is there. Flora treaded lightly and asked if such elaborate measures are necessary for two tomato plants and a few green peppers? At this, Donald tells Flora that here in the wild, subtropical climate of Florida, it is entirely necessary to protect ones produce from the exotic vermin that lay just beyond their hedge in the jungle. Wide- eyed, she immediately retreated to the safety of the patio. Case closed.

On the first Wednesday of each month, Flora elected to join a book club, which she tried to attend with some regularity, thinking it was a good way to make new friends in her golf and country club community. Two weeks later on club day, after a stimulating discussion on the book of the month and a sumptuous lunch at the club house, Flora returned home to find her husband beset with glee. She laughed at his boyish behavior and asked what on earth had him so tickled? As she laid down her purse, he gently took her by the arm and escorted her outside, waltzing her across the yard toward the enclosure he had built. With a beaming face, he opened the gate and bowing at the waist, motioned for her to go inside with the gallant gesture of his swooping arm. As she walked inside she squawked, her hands brought to her mouth to muffle her astonishment. There, huddled in the corner of Donald's ten-by-ten boxed enclosure was a Dartmoor sheep.

In total wonder she advanced on the young lamb, bent down and rubbed its wooly coat and began to laugh hysterically. "What have you done, you madman?" Flora chided Donald, as he joined her in fondling the baby sheep. "Donald you know you cannot house a sheep within a gated community, what were you thinking?" She choked out, as she began to laugh all over again.

"I'll tell ya what I was thinking," said Donald. "I was thinking DOG!"

"What do you mean, 'dog,'" asked Flora, a look of surprise peaking her brows. Donald went on to explain that all their neighbors had at least one, if not two dogs that they walked up and down the street on a leash; and that really, one man's dog could be another man's sheep, as long as the sheep looked like a very furry dog. By this time Flora was holding her sides trying to suppress more laughter, so the neighbors wouldn't hear and come to investigate. Flora was further amazed when out of Donald's old jacket pocket, he pulled a dog collar and lead.

"Darling" Donald said, "Do you remember when you were a child and had a pet lamb named Buggo?" Flora acknowledged that was true. "Well," he said, "Look at the name on the tag of the collar I bought." As she looked, she grinned, and again her hands flew to her mouth in astonishment.

"Oh, for heaven's sake Donald, I can't believe you have done this!" she replied. After an extended time of bonding, feeding and bedding down their new pet Buggo, Flora and Donald went inside to have some supper of their own and formulate a strategy for dealing with this secret new resident behind the gate.

After a few weeks of acclimation and growth, the time had come for a trial run; that meaning the dog Buggo was to launch out on his new lead for a promenade up and down the street of his cloistered community for the usual letting and exercise. After a quick brush of his fur and adjustment to his collar, Donald grabbed his pipe and walking stick and the two set out. It was a fine morning full of promise and the slight breeze added pleasure to their leisurely stroll up the sidewalk. Buggo, though still a lamb, with his long hair fluffing out nicely was not accustomed to a lead. From time to time, he would balk as he was encouraged to come along, but for the most part seemed happy enough to doddle about on his short little legs beside his master, taking in the sights. The first test came when Mrs. Arnold appeared on the street with her two high-strung, red Pomeranians. As Mrs. Arnold spotted Donald from afar, and commenced to wave and shout greetings, her two small dogs began to yap and strain at their leads in the direction of Buggo. The closer she got, the more her two small dogs went into frenzy, darting at Buggo, trying to pick up his scent. At the same time, Buggo stretched out his front legs, put his head down and bucked, kicking his hind legs at the yapping intruders. Mrs. Arnold finally reigning in her animals, looked perplexed, as she asked Donald what breed of dog he had, commenting she had never seen such a dog as his.

Donald, pulling Buggo up tight beside him and fluffing his fur, proudly proclaimed the beast to be a Scottish Highland sheep dog, a rare breed from the Isle of Skye in the Hebrides. At that Mrs. Arnold chuckled and said, "Darned if he doesn't look like a dog in sheep's clothing," and with that Donald cocked his head to one side and said, "Aye lass," and with a big broad smile, he bade her good day.

Life can often be uncertain and treacherous at best, for those on the slippery slope of temptation that often leads to degradation and hopelessness, even death. What seemed quite innocent at the time can ultimately end up ruling our lives. There is however, one sure way for the lost to be found and the hurting to be restored. Rebecca, who had spent herself on wild living, was now having to pay the price. Read about her miraculous salvation in **My Redeemer Lives**.

MY REDEEMER LIVES

One Sunday morning in 2013, I was listening to our pastor, a Masonic Jew for Christ, give a dynamic sermon on the vagaries of sin and the proverbial slippery slope that can lead to destruction. I became very engaged with the graphic picture he was painting of our current culture that seems to be plagued with satisfying the passions of every moment, never realizing the consequences of living with such choices. As the pastor went on, he talked about people who come to Florida to visit and return home with a baby alligator or python snake. He pointed out how novel and fun it could be to have such an exotic creature in an apartment in New York City. The problem is that these creatures do not remain small for very long, but soon outgrow their bath tub or aquarium and become harder to handle and more demanding to feed. Because our church was located in Deland, Florida, we all chuckled at these remarks about our northern friends until the pastor made a deadly analogy that wasn't so funny. He compared these exotic creatures to the temptations out in the world that seem fun and harmless at first, then grow, become more demanding and eventually life threatening. Very often the thing we so enjoy playing with comes to dominate our time and resources to the point we end up being in bondage to them. They begin to take over our lives and when it seems too late to make better choices, there seems to be no way out. The images the pastor described were so compelling, that on Monday morning, I sat up in my bed and felt driven to write something down about what I had heard. The following words of inspiration are what flowed from my pen.

She no longer realized where she was or how she had gotten there. Her faded, tattered, blue jeans, with the peek-a-boo designer holes along each leg, were now crusted with dirt and stains. The t-shirt she wore that had once been white was now smudged with grime from the streets and torn at the left shoulder. Her back ached as she tried to right herself with scratched, thin arms that revealed collapsed veins and faded tattoos. Her dirty, streaked, blond hair, cut in a short bob barely covered her ears and now fell across her face. She swiped at the greasy strands to clear her eyes as she raised her head to survey her surroundings. Her large, blue eyes nested in deep sockets on her bony face were surrounded by dark circles of delicate, thin flesh that twitched wildly as she tried to focus. Tossed out like so much trash, she wondered how long she had been out in the alley. She crawled to the nearest brick wall and sat there leaning while she stretched her legs and tried to make sense of her situation. Her purse, a quilted rag bag, was no longer with her. It had held just a few personal items, her ID, and some loose change piled in a corner of its one large gaping pocket. That shoulder bag had been her only constant companion since the day she bought it at the Salvation Army store for two dollars, more than five years ago, and now it was gone. Yes, even it was now gone, the last reminder of who she was.

Resting her weary head against the dark, worn brick wall of the alley, she allowed one single, large, crystal tear to escape her brimming eyes and roll to the hollow of her cheek. Through the heavy fog of drugs and alcohol she had consumed earlier, she now understood with gut wrenching clarity she had come to the end of her rope. The rope she had increasingly tightened around her own neck that was now choking the very life out of her body, soul, and spirit. The demon of addiction had taken sweet, young smiling Rebecca to places and with people she could never have anticipated. She took her first hit with a giggle, reveling in the excitement of anticipation, with the total acceptance of her peers, who were also likewise engaged. At the tender age of sixteen, the whole idea of doing something a little bit daring just for fun seemed innocent enough at the time. Now five years later at the ripe old age of twenty-one, she was totally spent and used up. The fights with her parents, dropping out of school and stealing to support her habits had landed her on the streets sooner than her young life was prepared for. What she had been forced to do, with people who had no names or faces, just to stay alive, had eventually killed her soul. She now wanted peace from it all. She wanted to die!

Bowing her head down between her trembling knees, she shook all over with anguish and that is when she heard it. At first, there was a slight breeze that arose in the alley, swirling old papers and leaves that had collected in its narrow passage, then the voice asked, "Daughter, why are you crying?" She looked up and saw a man staring down at her whose face was radiant with a warmth and tenderness she had never known. Next, he reached out his hands to her and literally lifted her to her feet. His deep brown almond eyes pierced the depth of her heart with a love so overwhelming she could not speak but instead stood transfixed in the moment. The rapture of his embrace melted away the grief and sorrow she had lived with for so many years. Her tortured mind began to clear through a whisper of remembrance of a sweeter time, when she was younger, bubbling with the joy of life and a hidden knowledge of God, that was tucked away deep within her spirit. Next, she heard her own voice cry out, "Jesus, Jesus!" and then it was over, this revelation of grace and mercy from a loving Savior. As Rebecca stood there alone in the alley filled with shock and wonder, another gust of wind picked up the dust, papers and leaves and deposited a shred of torn paper at her feet. Its edges were frayed, discolored with age and smudged with what looked like dried blood on the text. Feeling oddly compelled, Rebecca leaned down and picked up the paper to read a small group of words that were still legible. The passage read, *"So do not fear, for I am with you; do not be dismayed, for I am your God. I will strengthen you and help you; I will uphold you with my righteous right hand."* (Isaiah 41:10, NIV)

What happened over the next twenty-four hours was nothing short of a true miracle. Rebecca staggered through the streets of a neighboring community and then home to the town where she had grown up. As she approached her childhood home, she was acutely concerned about her disheveled appearance but soon found those emotions overridden by the overwhelming desire for wholeness that now seemed to drive her. As she climbed the stairs and stood on the porch at the front door, she took in a deep breath and with a trembling hand reached out to ring the bell. Oddly enough, both of Rebecca's parents arrived from different areas of the house to answer the call of the bell at the same time. When the door was opened, three people stood staring into one another's eyes in unspeakable shock and amazement. No one spoke or moved for the first few moments, as the total unexpected surprise registered in their minds. Then, collectively, arms were opened wide and Rebecca was clutched to the bosom of her mother and father, as tears of love, regret and relief freely flowed from their eyes. The Good Shepherd had left his flock and gone in search of the one who was lost. He will also come for you and me.

After writing this story, I felt more than ever, the redeeming grace of God that makes all things possible. In the history of the world, there has never been any other religious icon who is a living agent of change and restoration in people's individual lives but the one and only savior Jesus Christ. This story was a witness to my own spirit of the ongoing glory of God, yesterday, today, and forever. We are seen, known and loved. Then, just a day later after writing this story, something totally astounding happened that I will never forget.

It was a misty, damp morning. As I went outside to retrieve the trash can that had been emptied earlier, I noticed a couple of scraps of paper on the ground that the garbage man had missed, so I went to pick them up. One was a scrap from a newspaper ad and the other was a small piece of paper with a short, type written message on it. It simply said, "Romans 8:29." I could not believe it. Who finds a scripture reference in the street near trash cans? How does that happen? Then I remembered my story and the girl in the alley who received a confirmation from God that was just for her at that critical moment in her life. A shiver ran down my spine as I dashed to the house and grabbed my Bible. When I looked up the reference, I was astounded at the power and beauty of the verse. It said, "For those God foreknew he also predestined to be conformed to the likeness of his Son, that he might be the first born among many brothers." How awesome! It was the entire plan of salvation for mankind in one sentence. God, who knows us, has designed us to be like Christ and follow him into the resurrection for salvation … eternal life with God! Ironically, like the girl in my story, God had stepped into my life that day with his real presence, leaving me a love note, reassuring me of his existence and the peace and joy he longs to give all those who are willing to follow him.

ABOUT THE AUTHOR

Janice McLeod is a retired interior designer who currently resides in Ardmore, Oklahoma, a city near the beautiful Arbuckle Mountains. Janice has traveled extensively, living in many areas of the United States and abroad in Europe. She brings her special insights of experience and perception into play, as she now uses her creative energy to write short stories. Janice has always been fascinated by the knowledge that we are all so different and unique as individuals, yet so alike in our collective humanity, which is reflected in her work and creates the foundation for her new book *Beyond the Horizon: Chance Encounters with God.*